THE 10-MINUTE BUSINESS OWNER

THE 10-MINUTE BUSINESS OWNER

Experience Freedom, Build Wealth, and Create A LIFE WORTH LIVING

MARK EVANS DM

THE 10-MINUTE BUSINESS OWNER

Experience Freedom, Build Wealth, and Create a Life Worth Living

ISBN 978-1-5445-1121-4 *Paperback*

978-1-5445-1120-7 *Ebook*

A very special thank you to...

My amazing wife, Deena, who pushes me daily to be the best husband, father, and person I can be and our son Mark III, who has given me a big reason to make this world a better place... Your future is what drives me every day. I love you both so much.

My parents for making me! Seriously, my parents gave me life and the gifts to become who I am today. They are the hardest-working and most caring people I have ever known.

My grandmother, who was an amazing person, a huge part of my life, and a tremendous influence on my success.

All the mentors in my life, big and small, who have helped me realize there is so much to accomplish out there.

And my teams. You guys and gals are rock stars! I thank you for showing up daily and keeping the laser focus you have.

To the DM family... You all have no idea how much you mean to me.

To you, the reader...for investing in yourself. Enjoy the journey!

CONTENTS

I'm especially happy to dedicate 100 percent of the net profits from this book to the following charities: the Caring House Project Foundation, the Addison Quinn Foundation, the Lorraine Boys and Girls Club, and other missions that inspire me.

INTRODUCTION

From a young age, I learned to focus on the things I was good at and delegate to others what I was not good at. That's how Virgin is run. Fantastic people throughout the Virgin group run our businesses, allowing me to think creatively and strategically.

—RICHARD BRANSON, ENGLISH BUSINESS MAGNATE, INVESTOR, AND PHILANTHROPIST

"How the hell did I get here?"

That's what I ask myself as I sit comfortably on a beach chair, basking under the warm sunshine on the white, sandy beaches of an exclusive Caribbean island while the captain and crew of the yacht are in the distance preparing lunch for my family. As we wait, there's a fine local beer in my hand and an even finer cigar in my mouth.

I'm a long way from my days as a micromanaging business

owner in Columbus, Ohio, where I foolishly tended to every issue, large or small, from unresponsive sales leads to particularly nasty paper jams in the copy machine. This tropical island paradise is an even longer way from the trailer park of the small town I grew up in. Of course, in the middle of all that were two separate occasions when I nearly went bankrupt. So yes, this is good, but it's been a long and winding road to get here.

I've gone from barely graduating high school to making more money than I ever dreamed possible while traveling the world. Life is good, and it keeps getting better. Today, I'm on top of the world, running two successful, global businesses—a massive real estate investment firm and a lucrative media company—that generate millions of dollars each per year. Sure, the money is nice, but I also get to run my operation from anywhere in the world, which provides me with two other riches life has to offer: time and freedom!

So how did I get here? Keep reading and you'll find out.

Not every day is like today, when I get to sit beachside reflecting on my past, present, and future, with my lovely wife at my side and my son Mark III playing in crystal clear waters.

In fact, although my micromanaging days as a business

owner were more than twelve years ago, they're still fresh in my mind. As a young entrepreneur, I knew I had to hustle back then by working harder and longer than everyone else. Maybe you feel the same way, but everybody needs to work hard in the beginning. There comes a point, however, when you just don't have to do everything on your own anymore. In fact, there comes a point when you're losing money if you try to. The key is to know when you can start letting go.

Some days, I'm still in all-day conferences, but the God's honest truth is that on most days, I spend a total of about ten minutes in each of my businesses and continue to create multi-million-dollar returns.

I can hear you calling, "BS!" loud and clear from thousands of miles away, but it's true. It didn't happen overnight, and I had to work very hard to get here, but I did get here. Now, I'd like to share my story with you so that maybe it will help you to find your own way through the trials and tribulations of a micromanaging business owner to real freedom. I don't know everything, but I know what worked for me, and I know it can work for you too.

With the lessons I've learned about sustainable growth and how to let go of routine tasks—among other things—I'm confident that I can shave years off the learning curve for anyone who is willing to dive deep and do the work.

HIGH SCHOOL DAZE

As I finish a satisfying puff of my cigar and wash it down with my beer, I put my head back and reflect more deeply on how I got here. I surely wasn't the best student. In high school I didn't see the point of most of the things we studied, so I used to challenge and piss off my teachers on a fairly regular basis. I wasn't a bad kid—a class clown maybe—but I didn't do drugs, and I mostly stayed out of serious trouble. I just didn't see the point in memorizing a bunch of meaningless facts or acquiring some basic administrative skills that I had no intention of leveraging in the future.

I recall one teacher telling me that I had the attitude of a loser and wouldn't amount to anything because I didn't understand that everyone needs to get a real job in life. Yet even in those days, I knew there was money to be made, and that's what always interested me more than anything else. Deep down, I knew that I wanted to work for myself. My philosophy was that I would rather work a hundred hours a week for myself than forty hours for anybody else. I trusted in myself and just tuned the rest out.

Somehow, I managed to graduate high school...barely. After graduating, I bought my first business—a small seamless gutter company. I had virtually no money, but that was just an obstacle like many others that needed to be overcome. Fortunately, the previous owner, Larry, was willing to be creative with the financing, so he acted as the bank, and I paid him $287 per month for ownership of the business.

I did jobs for a lot of customers who would show up in high-end Porsches and who smoked expensive cigars. No matter how many times I saw these guys, I remained impressed by the lifestyle, so I made it a personal objective to find out how they got where they were. One day, I struck up a conversation with one of them, "Dude, nice car! What is it you do for a living, anyway?"

He told me he was a real estate investor. "I work a lot, but I make my own schedule, and I decide how the work gets done. Plus, I get to buy some cool toys, so yeah, it's a pretty good deal."

It turned out a lot of the other customers were also in real estate investing. I've never been the kind of person to get an idea and not act on it, so not long afterward, I started plotting how I was going to buy properties and make money...with virtually no money of my own!

I made my first real estate deal days before my nineteenth birthday. After that, it didn't take long before I started making deals pretty frequently. The problem was I was constantly running from one deal to the next while putting out every little brush fire that spontaneously combusted along the way. Truthfully, some of these fires could have been easily avoided if I hadn't been so distracted with trying to take care of every little detail on my own. I needed help, but I was too stubborn, proud, and ignorant to get it.

Any group of business owners I've ever been part of will undoubtedly involve at least a few of us chuckling over how busy we are. Someone will almost always use the firefighter analogy, as if all we do all day is put out fires. My perspective is just the opposite. We're not the firefighters—we're the arsonists! All those fires are there because we put them there, and then we feel like heroes when we put them out, which is ridiculous. There is a different way of getting business done. It's by being focused on our leadership and delegating the little things so that one or more of those little things don't ignite into a full-fledged warehouse fire.

A PIVOTAL MOMENT

October 8th, 2005, my grandmother died, which was a key point in my life because we had a great relationship, and she had a big impact on my life. I'll cover the details of this pivotal moment a little more in Chapter Two, but for now, just understand that it caused me to do some deep internal thinking about who I was and where I was going in life.

I wasn't making a lot of money at the time compared to what I make today, but I was still financially comfortable. Time, however, was a big problem because I didn't have enough of it, so I asked myself some important questions.

Why bother being in business at all if I'm going to be running around like a maniac chasing everything down on my own, just to maintain a comfortable status quo? What's the point of working so hard if I don't have any time to enjoy it?

A few months later, my wife (girlfriend at the time), Deena and I were in my office late one night. I was used to starting work at 4:00 a.m. and leaving at 11:00 p.m. because I thought I loved it, and let's be honest, I never felt like I had enough time in the day. As business owners, we feel like our work is never done, right? That fateful night, however, I stayed even later, and Deena joined me because she wanted to spend some time with me, which was hard to come by because I worked so much. But that night, I wasn't doing much work.

I was still hurting from my grandmother's recent passing, so I was doing some deep soul-searching instead, thinking about how short life really is. It made me realize I was tired of working such ludicrous hours every day, overanalyzing every tedious task of business minutiae that landed on my desk. There were other things I wanted to do with my life. I wanted to do some traveling and spend more time with my family and friends.

Finally, I said, “Enough is enough.”

Deena understood where my mental state was at, and that night, we devised a plan for me to start letting go of some of the insanely overwhelming administrative tasks related to my business. “Let’s get the hell out of Columbus for a while to unwind,” she suggested. At first, I wondered how the hell she thought I was going to be able to do that because I had so much work to do, but rather quickly, I realized the idea wasn’t so crazy. In fact, it was exactly what I needed to do. With that in mind, I somewhat painfully decided to put the day-to-day operations of my business in the capable hands of my team in Ohio while Deena and I took off for a month to South Beach, Florida.

LETTING GO

With a semi-devised plan in place to let go of my micromanaging nature, we embarked on a journey that ended up changing everything for me. I put all the administrative tasks and routine aspects of operating my business in the hands of my team.

“So, what happened?” you ask.

Did my office burst into flames the first time the phone rang with a critical situation that I was unavailable to tend to in person? Was the lunch hour replaced with happy hour, featuring ninety-nine-cent cocktails and ten-cent wings? Did my team start looting the office like it was some sort of post-apocalyptic free-for-all?

Nope, none of those things happened. What did happen was that my team became empowered to do things on their own, which actually led to far more efficient daily operations. Now, I would be lying to you if I said things went smooth as silk, but I can tell you that most of what went wrong wasn't catastrophic by any means. Could I get on the phone and close a deal better than anyone in the office? Yes. Chances are, you can sell your product better than anyone else as well, but there is no scale in that.

Meanwhile, my time was freed up tremendously. I enjoyed a level of freedom I never had before. I didn't have to spend so much time thinking about the small details of my work. It was also an opportunity to commit some time to create a vision and think bigger about my business. The simple act of letting go opened the door to eventually expand my business to a level that would have never been possible otherwise.

It wasn't easy at first. In fact, I definitely experienced some nasty withdrawal symptoms during the initial transition period. I had anxiety so severe that it led to full-scale panic attacks with sleepless nights, chest pain, and dry heaving. Eventually, however, as things fell into place, it all became worth it and then some.

One more thing happened. Things went so well that our one-month trip to Florida turned into a brand-new lifestyle. Once we realized that I could run my business from anywhere, we toured the world. Over the next two and a half years, I virtualized my entire business, and the industry soon followed suit.

Traveling forced me to let go of my tendency to be a control-freak business owner. I wholeheartedly recommend it as an impetus for your own trial run of letting go. Find the one or two things you're truly great at as an entrepreneur and hire good people to take care of the rest.

By traveling, I don't mean pack up the SUV to go fishing at the lake that's a couple of hours away. I mean go somewhere far enough away so that you can't just hop on a plane and be home within a couple hours, and stay there for a minimum of two weeks. It takes at least that long to really decompress from the rigors of running almost every aspect of your business.

Before I traveled that first time, I was riding a roller coaster of emotions from overwhelmed, scared, and sad to grateful, optimistic, happy, and positive, as well as everything in between. Clarity was at a premium. Perhaps it was even nonexistent.

I recommend taking this moment to write down some of the things you might be feeling. Get out a pencil and paper and draw a line down the middle. On one side, write down the positive things you're feeling. On the other, write down some of your negative emotions. Try to get at least ten emotions on each side. When you're done, try to really understand each one of them (where they come from, what they mean, etc.) and decide if a journey somewhere far away may help you to gain some clarity as well. I'm almost sure that after you give your list some thought, you'll come to the same conclusion I did, which is that it's time to decompress and let go a little.

FOCUSED ACTION

As a business owner, it's easy to get caught up in the weeds of your everyday business routines. Believe me, nobody was more deeply entangled in them than I was. It's extremely important to get out of there because being buried down there distorts your vision, which is most likely one of your best assets. After all, you chose to be an entrepreneur because you had a big-picture idea and wanted to have an impact on the world, not because you wanted to punch a time clock and make widgets on an assembly line all day. That sort of job is fine, but let's face facts: it's not who you are.

You don't need to present at every client meeting, and the deal isn't going to go south just because you weren't on a conference call with the rest of the team. Realize that your time is the most valuable commodity you have in life. You need to take focused action on everything you do. Start by asking yourself some of the following questions the next time you're in a conference or on a phone call:

- Who are you talking to and why?
- What are the action steps that will result from this conversation?
- What critical information, if any, are they sharing with you, and what does it mean?
- Could you have hired someone else to take care of this interaction just as competently as you can?
- Is this call or anything related to the conversation, replicable?
- Is this a call that can be recorded and used as reference for a similar circumstance in the future?

The answer to the last question is almost certainly yes, and I don't care who you are or how valuable you think your presence is. Bill Gates doesn't need to be on the phone every time someone can't get Outlook to send a group email to the right recipients.

The key is hiring the right people and putting them in the best possible situation to leverage their inherent strengths to succeed. More on that later, but bringing talented people on board is one way that will allow you—the business owner—to take focused action.

Remember, you can't run a big business with a small mindset!

FEAR OF LOSING CONTROL

As business owners, we are wired to attempt controlling as much as possible. I had to learn how to let go of my nature as a control freak, and you probably do too. It's easy to get frustrated when you're working too many hours, like I was, but I don't think a lot of us ask the right questions when that happens, including myself. Until I started to let go, I was always asking something like, "When the hell will I get to the point where I don't have to do this shit anymore?" The question I should have been asking myself, however, was, "How can this shit get done without me being involved every time?" Or, "How can I pay someone else to do it?" That is a much more focused question, and it struck at the core of my problem, which was that I needed to address my fear of losing control. I finally realized I was the effing problem.

The key to letting go is hiring team players with the goal of getting A-list talent on board to run the less important aspects of your business and empowering them with solid decision-making abilities. Truthfully, these people are more capable of doing things like administrative tasks, paperwork, and other routine operations because that's who they are. Of course, this concept isn't as simple as it might sound because I didn't have any idea what a top-performing team member even looked like in the beginning. How would I? I had never seen one before because I just did everything myself.

Spotting A-list talent—as hard to find as they are—is a process just like anything else, but you have to learn from your mistakes. Once you start learning, you'll find plenty of highly capable people to work for you. Most of them won't be A-listers, at least in the beginning, because those people are a rare find. But if you look hard enough and invest in them appropriately, a few of them might become A-listers.

Depending on what the job description is, it's perfectly acceptable to hire C to B (average to slightly above average) workers for your business. Be careful not to sell these people short though or to pigeonhole them into being mediocre workers forever. With the right coaching, leadership, training, and development, they could rise to the level of A-lister someday as well. That's the goal. Get the right person for the job and empower them with whatever is necessary to perform at the highest level they're capable of.

After you find the best people you can to help you run your business, it's up to you to pay them, invest in their growth, and enable them to succeed. For instance, I hire a lot of salespeople today, and some of them are definitely A-listers, but I have to enable them to succeed by hiring sales trainers and getting them the information they need. I pay for them to get educated and stay that way. A-list talent needs to not just be acquired; it needs to be nurtured.

WORK *ON* YOUR BUSINESS, NOT *IN* IT

Key Performance Indicators (KPI) – This is the data that matters most for your company. KPIs are a performance measurement. They are the numbers that help you to determine successes and failures while also helping you to make decisions on where to focus your efforts best.

Ask yourself, are you the visionary *and* the implementer? If so, stop and hire some people who implement much more effectively/consistently than you can. Once you do that, you'll discover there is a big difference between working *on* a business and working *in* a business.

Working *in* your business means you're in the office or in the field for way too many hours every day, micromanaging every aspect of it. Conversely, working *on* your business means something much less routine. You could be anywhere in the world planning the next big deal you're going to make. Maybe you'll be thinking about a new hire to grow the company, working on KPIs to know what is working and what isn't, or planning the next acquisition for growth. Or you could be working on your overall vision to continue growing the company. That's where you want to be—working *on* the business, not *in* it.

Not every business day will involve a mere ten minutes of work from an exotic island locale, but you can definitely work a lot less and make much more from anywhere in the world. After all, the internet has made virtual business much easier, and I wholeheartedly endorse using it to your advantage.

If this book gets you from working twelve hours in the office every day down to four, or ten down to three, that is a major victory to me! Someday you might even get it down to an hour or two, then a half-hour, and eventually ten minutes. Who knows? Maybe soon, you and I will share a beer and a cigar together while talking business on the sandy beaches of a tropical island resort and watching our kids play in the water. If I can do this, I bet you can too.

You might be thinking that I'm asking you to run away from your business. That would be foolish, and it's not something I would ever recommend. Instead, I'm telling you to work on freeing up mind time to work *on* the business (not *in* it) and grow it.

WHAT THIS BOOK IS AND IS NOT

What you're about to read is not a clunky textbook, filled with step-by-step instructions about how to implement process efficiencies A, B, and C. There will be no word-for-word, sure-fire sales pitches, nor will there be any microanalyzed marketing campaigns, motivational tactics, or any other ground-level aspects of your business. One more disclaimer of sorts: this book is also not intended for anybody just starting out as a business owner. You will find no information about how businesses get off the ground, start making money, and establish themselves as an industry presence.

None of those things are my areas of expertise in the island life as the Deal Maker and Digital Nomad. I've been through the ringer in building my business. I worked long days and nights while experiencing all the emotional turmoil that comes with getting a business up and running. Thankfully, I don't have to think about those things anymore, but I will always have to think about how to continue growing my business, and that's what I'm here to help you with. After all, plenty of great books have already been written about how to establish a business. This one's a little different. It's about how to take that business to new heights while exponentially enhancing your own lifestyle.

This book is intended for the established entrepreneur or

business owner. It is a high-level piece that shares some thoughts and approaches to further growth and success that worked for me but that I'm certain can work for any business. You are about to learn about many big-picture ideas, thoughts, and high-level approaches that I've seen work for advancing your business and lifestyle.

You'll also learn some common missteps we all tend to gravitate toward as business owners and how to avoid them. I've made plenty of mistakes along the way, but I learned from them, and now I want to share them with you, so maybe you won't have to endure the same problems I did.

One of the biggest mistakes I made, and most business owners make, is thinking that I had to do everything myself. The truth is nobody should sustain that, and if you are, you're placing unnecessary limitations on your business and your life, just like I was. Perhaps most importantly, you'll learn how you can and need to let go of all the necessary evils of running a business, like administrative and routine operational tasks. Once you come to the realization of letting go, and do it, the sky is the limit! Working less and making more isn't smoke and mirrors. It's very real, and all you need to get started is to keep reading.

CHAPTER ONE

MAKE MONEY, BUY TIME, BE FREE

A business that makes nothing but money is a poor business.

—HENRY FORD, FOUNDER OF FORD MOTOR COMPANY

I'd like to provide a small bit of additional context to that pivotal moment in 2005 when Deena and I first decided to pack our bags for Florida.

I was only twenty-seven years old, but I had been a business owner since I graduated high school, so I already had nine years of business experience under my belt. Nonetheless, I still had youth on my side, so I had plenty of time to become the person I envisioned myself being someday. Shortly before we made the decision to travel, and as my mind was going through the soul-searching process inspired by my grandmother's passing,

I wrote some things down that I wanted, and noticed a common theme.

- I want to make more money.
- I want to have a bigger impact on the world.
- I want to be free to pursue my life purpose.
- I want to grow my business from anywhere in the world.
- I want *time* and *financial freedom.*

All those things told me that I needed to think beyond just being *rich* in terms of money to accomplish my goals. I needed to be *rich* in terms of money *and* time.

WHAT IT REALLY MEANS TO BE RICH

If you ask most people why they're in business, they'll have a quick answer, which is that they want to be rich. But what does it really mean to be rich?

To me, money is a critical tool that allows me to buy time and, ultimately, freedom. Money lets me spend quality time with my family, share some laughs with my friends, and hopefully be a good steward to the world around me. For that reason, money is a very important aspect of not just business but life as well. We need to make money so we can invest in ourselves. By that, I mean we should use money to buy time and freedom, which are also extremely valuable commodities.

I had lunch the other day with a guy who generates around $50 million per year. He told me he is not letting up until he has $100 million in his bank account. I thought to myself, "Man, you're looking at the wrong number. You barely even know your kids' names, and when was the last time you took your wife out to dinner? For that matter, anytime I have seen you eating dinner with your family, the phone is glued to your ear. What good is that? The game of life isn't just about money. It's about time. You need to use more of that money to buy yourself some time, my friend." Then again, his definition of rich may be different than mine. Quite often, he jokingly says, "Mark, I want to be like you when I grow up. You're always hanging out in shorts and flip-flops."

If it sounds like I have a tough-love approach with people, you're spot on, but I really believe it's what people need to hear sometimes. It always comes from a good place—not anger or hostility—but more out of compassion and servitude.

If you're out there working like a dog just to watch the numbers in your bank account grow, you're losing at the game of life, as far as I'm concerned. I've never heard anyone who is preparing to die say something like, "Man, I wish I had five more bucks in my pocket for when they put me in the ground." That would be ridiculous. However, I have heard plenty of people in that situation say something like, "I wish I had spent more time with my family." Others may say something like, "I wish I had traveled more or made a bigger impact on the people I really care about."

Regret comes in all different flavors, but every one of them tastes bitter. Money will buy you time to have the freedom to do what you want and live without regret, or at least with less of it. That's why the game of life is also about time, not necessarily all about money.

WHAT DOES REAL FREEDOM LOOK LIKE?

Some people see freedom as not having debt, and that's a fine mentality to have, but it's not the whole picture because there is good debt and bad debt.

Another term for good debt is "passive income," which is earnings you don't have to work for to create. It could be from a rental property, limited partnership, or investment. A great way to begin creating passive income is to increase your financial knowledge. Read some books on investing. Listen to financial podcasts. Read articles online. There is a wealth of information out there to help you make money without busting your hump. All you need is to invest your time wisely to figure out how to do it. Remember, we're either spending our time or investing it. A good book to learn more about this is *Rich Dad,*

Poor Dad by Robert Kiyosaki. The more I learn about how money really works, the more I make and keep. It's a never-ending journey, but it's a fun one and definitely one worth learning more about.

One idea is to gamify passive income. For instance, you could ask yourself, "How do I get a free car?" Once you create enough passive income that pays for the car payment, try something else, like how to get a free house, and so on.

The reason most people don't do this is because something like a car payment is small numbers ($500 per month) to a business owner. By gamifying it, however, you're challenging yourself, which is something most of us can definitely relate to.

Once you acquire enough passive income, real freedom presents itself because you no longer need to show up at the office to make money. How you take advantage of that precious reward is entirely up to you.

I created a company—American Wealth Builders—whose mission is to help people create passive income through real estate cash flow assets. It's a great resource to begin your own quest for passive income, and if you're interested in creating double-digit returns, you can download the *free* report here: www.AmericanWealthBuilders.com/10.

Bad debt, however, is something you definitely want to eliminate. Some examples of bad debt are the house you live in, most cars, boats, and other similar items. With very few rare exceptions, those things aren't going to make you any money.

Freedom from debt is a noble notion, but you need to classify it into good and bad. Getting rid of the bad and keeping the good is a simple enough concept, but it's also easy enough to overlook. Fear of acquiring any kind of debt can cause people to not pull the trigger on an idea or big deal that could make a lot of money.

You need to be careful at this moment because real freedom can be a scary transition if you're not ready for it. At this level of success, most of us don't *need* to work as much as we *want* to work. Boredom is a huge problem for a lot of business leaders, athletes, celebrities, and others. Some of us struggle with depression early on because we're not big enough, successful enough, or wealthy enough. Then, a strange thing happens when we achieve all those things. It's a shock to the system, and we start to wonder what's next. That's what happened to me. I was depressed and felt lost and overwhelmed often when I was trying to get my business off the ground because of all those things I hadn't yet achieved. Then, when I achieved all those things I wanted and stepped away from the business, I finally gained real freedom, but I also had no idea what to do with it at first.

This transition caused me some major depression. It felt like I lost my identity when I didn't have to show up for work all day anymore. They say idle hands are the devil's workshop, and I definitely found that to be true. I'm happy to say that I figured it out eventually, and I'm sure you will too. For me, I just needed to realize that the amazing opportunity I had with all this free time shouldn't be wasted. I realized there was no point to all this freedom if I was wasting it by taking on bad behaviors, so I started using it more effectively by spending more time with family and friends and creating profitable, passion-driven businesses.

Now, I travel and enjoy my life to the fullest, but I had to go through those dark times to get here. I feel like if I was more prepared for the complex emotions of real freedom, I could have avoided some of that depression that set in. Maybe by explaining it this way, I can help you to be ready for it and embrace the opportunity from the outset. Now that you're aware of this potential pitfall, you can take some comfort in knowing you're not alone. We all fight silent battles within ourselves, but you can also hire someone to help you navigate the stormy weather of emotions when necessary.

Real freedom, however, is something different. It's all about being able to do what you want, when you want, and with whom you want. What keeps most people from achieving freedom is getting too comfortable and falling in love with their daily work routine or the traditional path to retirement. You need to step outside of your comfort zone and embrace the discomfort because it means you're growing.

GET COMFORTABLE WITH BEING UNCOMFORTABLE

Originally, I got uncomfortable by traveling because it forced me to get away from the day-to-day tasks of running my business. By doing that, my schedule freed up to commit more focused action, think bigger, and live better. In fact, I traveled so much and made so many deals from abroad that I was given the term "Digital Nomad" (DN) in addition to my existing reputation as the "Deal Maker" (DM).

Later on, I stepped a little further outside of my comfort zone by going to *business* conferences and mastermind groups rather than exclusively *real estate* conferences. I saw this idea as a great investment in myself. If I can invest $10,000 for a two-day mastermind and walk away with hundreds of thousands in real value to implement, that return is a no-brainer. It was new to me then, but I leaned into it, and it continues to pay off with big returns to this day.

If you're cringing at the thought of investing tens of

thousands of dollars in self-development courses and knowledge programs, you're looking at it all wrong. Remember, you're not investing in the program—you're investing in yourself!

Rather than trying to justify committing to such an expense, you should think about why you wouldn't make such an investment. Don't immediately assume that the program is useless or not legitimate. That's a negative mindset, and it's not conducive to sustainable growth. Instead, think positively that you are buying useful information which will produce a consistently high rate of return for many years. Think of it as an education expense because you're going to leverage the knowledge from those programs and get a high rate of return that more than pays for the upfront cost. You get it or you wouldn't be investing your time in this book as it was an investment in money and time.

A lot of people go to the same industry conferences, in the same places, and network with the same people, which certainly has its place in the business world, but you should never limit yourself like that.

I had been to real estate conferences all over the world for many years, but real estate was something I was already good at, so I didn't need any more industry-specific knowledge. There was no need for me to learn the next trendy closing tactic, the newest investment strategy, or a cutting-edge sales technique. Most of those things had already been done before anyway.

The knowledge I really needed was how to build a better business. It's that type of foundational skillset that entrepreneurs often overlook in favor of industry-specific trends, and it's a mistake. At some point, you have to learn how to become a better business owner and leader if you're going to continue growing.

I UNDERSTAND. TRUST ME

A few years ago, a client named Joe, who was trying to balance being a broker and a real estate investor at the same time, sought my advice. He was never really a micromanager, but he was afraid to hire and leverage human capital, which was seriously stunting the growth of his business and his quality of life.

We became friends many years ago after Joe hired me. Over the years, we had many conversations about business and life, but this particular conversation is very appropriate for the topic at hand.

He started the conversation with, "I hate being a broker, Mark. I want to give it up so badly because I absolutely can't stand it anymore!" Fortunately for Joe, he was also running a successful investment company that was making him money, so he could afford to completely ditch the broker side of his business. Something that drastic wasn't necessary, and it wasn't the right move anyway.

Joe elaborated his point: "As a broker, I have to wear a suit and drive people around all day like a friggin' chauffeur. That sucks and it's a waste of time! Meanwhile, I can wear flip-flops and a T-shirt at my investment company, and nobody cares. Help me out, Mark. What should I do?"

I would later find out that Joe's distaste for being a broker was even more serious than he let on in that conversation. He was actually ready to shut down the company entirely. Fortunately, Joe kept an open mind, didn't do anything impulsive, and engaged in a conversation with me about how we might be able to fix his problem.

We began to exchange ideas about how he could separate himself from the broker side of his business, and eventually, I said, "Joe, you think you need to be there for everything your business does, but you don't. If you don't like driving people around, don't do it! Hand off all the things you hate about being a broker to someone else. Pay them well enough to do a great job, and don't waste any more time on the less important aspects you hate. Life's way too short for that."

Joe began his response by saying, "Yeah, but you don't understand—"

That's when I interrupted him because a lot of entrepreneurs and business leaders—like myself at one time—start their pushback at the notion of letting go with, "You don't understand..."

"BS!" I told him. "I do understand. You're the guy who doesn't understand. That's why you're fighting me about it. Next, you're going to tell me about how you're the face of your business, and it's crucial to the brand that your face is not only on all the postcards and front-lawn "For Sale" signs, but also at every showing, closing, and everything else. BS! The harsh truth is that it doesn't need to be like that at all."

I think it was the tone of certainty in my voice that got his attention, and he listened to what I had to say after that. Together, we further discussed how he could restructure his marketing and delegate all the personal interaction aspects of being a broker to qualified, trustworthy team members.

Eventually, I was able to share with Joe how to take a risk on his own people and let them take over the brokerage side of his business. Within a year, they were doing as well (almost better) than he did. When I asked him about this later on, he said that the lesson he learned was that there is great power in leveraging people.

Joe continued to market his brand very effectively after that, but by letting go of all the unnecessary face-time he hated so much about being a broker, he became much more successful in his business and infinitely happier in his personal life. It allowed him to think bigger, sustain growth, and achieve freedom.

Meanwhile, the brokerage side of his business never skipped a beat from the year he walked away from it. After building an awesome team, they were able to double the size of the company from one year to the next for four straight years. The brokerage side of his business went from a one-man show to a company of over twenty-five great team players and one of the top real estate teams in the state of New Jersey. This all happened and Joe still doesn't deal with any clients on a daily basis at all.

This aspect of trusting his people allowed him to completely let go of the vine on the brokerage side. His people now control the process on automation. It helped him to create a virtual business and walk away, which has created real freedom for him to start other companies and venture into other investments. Now, he spends most of his time working on himself, instead of in his business, and he helps others to do the same through events and mastermind groups. He also spends much more time with his family and is even writing his own a book about his journey in business.

Joe is now a good friend. However, in business, you need to find people who are able to separate coaching and mentorship from friendship.

A BEAUTIFUL CYCLE

It might sound corny, but we only get one shot at life, so why not make the most of it?

As business owners, sometimes we get unfairly misjudged. Other people think we're immune to everything of significance in life other than making money, but that's not true. I know plenty of other business owners who wisely value their time and freedom much more than money, but they're too afraid to let go of anything to get what they really want out of life.

My point is to not be afraid to get what you really want out of life. Use your money wisely to buy more time. Then, use that extra time to find real freedom. You'll discover there's a cyclical nature to that process, because with more time and freedom, you'll start to make more money, which allows one to steward at another level. It's a beautiful thing!

CHAPTER TWO

LIFE IS SHORT. DON'T SETTLE FOR LESS

I wish for a world where people understand that life is short. So, today's the time to do big things.

—ROBIN SHARMA, CANADIAN AUTHOR AND MOTIVATIONAL SPEAKER

Stage IV cancer with two weeks to live... That's the diagnosis my grandmother was given in 2005. This woman was tough as nails and the rock of my family, as well as a huge mentor to me growing up. She was completely fine as far as any of us knew until the day she went to the doctor for a routine checkup. That's when it hit us all like a ton of bricks—she only had about two weeks left to live.

I think she lived for about ten days beyond her initial diagnosis, as she passed away on October 8th, 2005. Therefore, time was of the essence for all of us who wanted to say goodbye. I remembered reading about regret in a book many years ago, and it stuck with me, so I was quite aware of how horrible regret can be to live with. I dropped everything as soon as I heard the news and made sure I told her how important she was to me and how much I loved her before it was too late.

There was one problem with opening up to her like that. I knew I would never be able to get the words out face-to-face without crying uncontrollably. There was no doubt in my mind that I would turn into a blubbering mess and never be able to say what I needed to, so I chose a different method to express my feelings for her.

I decided to write a heartfelt letter to my grandmother, carefully articulating what she meant to me, how much I loved her, and how she helped me become the man I am today. After I wrote the letter, I recorded myself reading it on a cassette player I had. When I went to see her at her house, which was where she wanted to pass, I sat beside her on the bed and played the recording for her. I held her hand tightly as we listened to it and cried together.

That was an incredibly special moment to me and one of the toughest things I've ever had to do in life. But I'm so glad I did it because it gave me the closure I desperately needed. I still miss my grandmother immeasurably today, but at least I don't have to live the rest of my life with regret, thinking, "I wish I would have told her how I felt before she died."

Since then, I've shared this approach with just about everybody I've ever spoken with who is about to lose a loved one, and over the years, I've heard some incredible stories that resulted from the process.

That story echoes the sentiment that life is not everlasting. As young men and women, we tend to think we're going to live forever, but in the back of our minds, we all know that's not true. At some point, we all have to stop lying to ourselves and understand we're not going to live forever, so why settle for anything less. You only have so much time in this world, so now is the time to make the most of it.

With that sudden awakening of how short life really is, many thoughts began to consume me. The thoughts weren't very consoling, but they were purposeful, and it may help you to think about them as well.

If you die tomorrow, what would be your legacy or impact on the world?

Would people remember you for what you did or what you didn't do?

When I die, I want there to be a celebration of my life, not a dour service. I want people to have fun discussing the positive impacts I made.

I don't want to die with regret of what I could have had, could have accomplished, or could have been in life.

From that moment on, I decided that I was never going to settle for anything less than what I wanted out of life, and there is no reason you should either.

LEVEL UP ACROSS THE BOARD

I always hated when people told me, "You should just be thankful for what you have." What the hell does that really mean? I am thankful for what I have, but I still want more. Just because I don't settle for complacency doesn't mean I don't appreciate all the great things I have in the present moment. It is possible to be grateful and want more out of life.

Before my grandmother's death, I was doing pretty well, financially speaking. But after that realization of how short life is, I thought about how much more was possible to get out of it, and there was no time like the present to go after it. That pivotal moment served as inspiration to level up across the board. If you're going for more out of life, you need to look and act the part. Therefore, I started wearing better clothes, going to nicer restaurants, and purchasing better equipment for my business.

It might sound a little trivial, but instead of wearing perfectly good Levi's for around $50 per pair, I started to buy nicer jeans for around $300 per pair. Do they feel a lot different? Sort of, but that's not the point. It was more about my evolution from the status quo to thinking bigger.

Truthfully, wearing $300 blue jeans with a custom-fit, professionally tailored dress shirt seemed a little awkward to me in the beginning because I wasn't sure I deserved it. Then, I realized it was about more than just the way the material felt or the way the design looked. It was about investing in myself, which is positively invaluable.

Plenty of people are perfectly happy with the status quo, but that's likely not you, and it's definitely not what this book is about.

Don't settle for inferior business systems either. Instead of taking the cheap way out by purchasing introductory-level business equipment and information systems, I started buying higher-quality items across the board for my business as well. I was smart about it. One paper clip is just as good any other, so I didn't buy titanium paper clips or anything like that, but I spared no expense on the things that mattered, like personnel and software.

Instead of hiring people who could just get me by with their average skillsets and average performance, I started a process designed to hire the A-list talent I mentioned earlier. They were harder to find and cost more money, but they were well worth it because they proved to be the biggest reason I was able to let go of the little things in my business and work remotely. In fact, top team players are so important to leveling up that I've included two chapters (7 and 8) dedicated to explaining how to do it. For now, just understand that hiring top talent isn't as easy as it sounds because I had to hire many B and C players to understand what an A player was. Maybe you're already there, but the goal is to get at least some A-list talent on board. Keep your eyes and your ears open because the diamond in the rough may surface anytime.

Ultimately, it was a combination of all those leveled-up aspects in my personal and professional life that made it possible for me to take that leap when I traveled to Florida with my then girlfriend, now wife, Deena. I simply refused to settle for less, demanded better, and had the systems and people in place to make it all happen. No matter what business you're in, you can do the same.

It helps if you can find like-minded people to form business relationships with. Most of us have an inner circle of friends and colleagues who feed off each other's energy. Therefore, you should associate with other business leaders and successful entrepreneurs who also demand better. An inner circle composed of such individuals will help to level up your own expectations.

Where do you find such a group of like-minded individuals to yourself? Start by going to www.10MinuteBusinessOwner.com for a checklist and some helpful videos that can expedite your journey.

SUCCESSFUL BUSINESSES NEED A VISIONARY AND AN IMPLEMENTER

When Apple was still emerging as a major player in the technology sector, it had two founders—Steve Jobs and Steve Wosniak. Jobs was always the idea man, the visionary, the big-picture guy. Meanwhile, Wosniak was always the doer, the implementer, the man who made it all happen. That's why their business relationship worked so well.

A partnership needs to have complimentary skillsets. One person has to be the visionary, and the other has to be the implementer because serious problems occur when two visionaries or two implementers try to work together. Both situations result in a stalemate because the visionaries will never get any actual work done, and two implementers won't know where to begin.

If you're in a partnership with two visionaries, you need

to have a conversation for the relationship to work out. Only one of you can be the "Steve Jobs" and the other one has to be the "Steve Wosniak." If the situation can resolve itself to provide both skills, then that business relationship has a serious chance to work quite well. If, however, both people seem to have overlapping skillsets and nobody appears willing to accept a different role, it might be best to call out the dysfunction and dissolve the partnership. In terms of the potential for wasted time and resources, you'll both be much better off in the long run.

Every case is different, so I'm not saying to call your partner and break up now. Your particular partnership could be working very well; in which case, it definitely makes sense to keep it going. I just want to call your attention to some of the potential pitfalls so you can carefully evaluate your partnership and make sure it's working.

Whenever two people from a potentially dysfunctional partnership approach me for advice, my first question is always, "Who runs the vision of your company?"

They usually have an awkward moment or two of silence and stare at each other for a few seconds before one of them sheepishly says something like, "Uh, well, we kind of both do."

To which, I usually respond, "Do you see a problem with

that? If that doesn't change or if someone isn't willing to step back from the company's vision and take on the role of implementer, your partnership has an inordinately high probability of self-destructing."

A clear vision backed by effective implementation will allow you to grow rapidly.

One important distinction to make is to not misunderstand my idea of leveling up with something I hear a lot of in today's business circles, which is the notion of taking massive relentless action.

MASSIVE RELENTLESS ACTION IS BS

Business leaders walk around talking about taking massive relentless action like it's some sort of secret success elixir. I'm calling BS on the whole idea, and here's why: most of the entrepreneurs I talk to have no problem with taking massive relentless action. It's in our DNA. In fact, most of us have been doing this our whole lives. It would seem impossible to get to the level of success most of us are at without working incredibly hard (at least in the early stages), but what a lot of us don't understand is that massive relentless action is only one side of the equation. Most of the people I know disregard the importance of focus when they take massive relentless action, but focus is the other key variable that must be present. For that reason,

I recommend disregarding massive relentless action as nothing more than a trending catchphrase. Massive relentless action without focus is death, and I see it daily!

In the next chapter, I'll explain how some of the problems you think you have in your business are not your real problems. Once you're able to identify the real problems, you'll be ready to work smarter, not necessarily harder, and the sky is the limit from there.

CHAPTER THREE

THE PROBLEMS YOU *THINK* YOU HAVE ARE NOT THE PROBLEMS YOU *ACTUALLY* HAVE

We can't solve problems by using the same kind of thinking we used when we created them.

—ALBERT EINSTEIN, GERMAN-BORN THEORETICAL PHYSICIST AND GENIUS

I don't wear suits, but years ago, while I was in the process of leveling up across the board, I decided to put one on for an important meeting with a marketing agency. There I was, Mr. Big Shot with a kick-ass designer suit and a manila folder chock-full of important documents in my left hand. Keep in mind, this was around 2000. Whereas all this stuff is in the cloud today, back then, files were still made of paper and kept in manila folders instead of being made of bits and bytes and stored on servers.

I was bursting with confidence and enthusiasm right out of my custom-fit shirt collar, thinking I was going to absolutely crush it at this meeting. In my mind, I was already sold on whatever they were going to tell me. Remember, I was leveling up across the board, so I knew I needed better salespeople, better systems, and better marketing to not just look more successful but be more successful.

"Just pay it," I was initially thinking to myself, because I knew whatever marketing budget increase they recommended would instill growth in my business. Unfortunately, that certainty in my mindset wouldn't last. I was already spending $10,000 per month with them, but now they were trying to sell me on the idea of raising the stakes to around $30,000 per month. That was when my bursting confidence quickly began to subside. Suddenly, my palms were getting a little sweaty, and my legs started shaking a bit. That's when I realized that money actually was a problem, but I was lying to myself that it wasn't in an effort to feel good about my situation.

In my head, I figured that if I spent three times as much in marketing, I'd reap three times the profits, but I couldn't be 100 percent sure of that. After all, that's a really simplistic way of analyzing a business decision because there was no quantifiable data behind it at this point in my business. I needed more than a not-so-educated guess at my return on investment (ROI) to make a big decision like that.

Was $100,000 the limit of what I was willing to spend, or was it only $10,000? Or was it somewhere in between? I'm not really sure, but I passed on the deal anyway, mostly because I was too scared and unprepared to make a good decision.

In the end, my decision to not pull the trigger was much more of a data problem than anything else. I didn't have the real numbers I needed to ensure my ROI would triple or even make up for the increased investment. I won't make that mistake again because now I understand the huge value of data in making business decisions. In fact, that moment of indecision led to a particularly meaningful motto of mine, which is "Data, not drama!"

MARK'S MOTTO #1: "DATA, NOT DRAMA"

In those days, I was spending a decent amount of money but had no data to justifiably back up any of it, so a $30,000 investment was too big a risk to attempt. Now, I realize that if I had the KPIs to tell me what my actual ROI would be, I would have been able to make a much more informed decision about my increased marketing budget.

To gain a much deeper understanding on the importance of KPIs for any business, I highly recommend the book *Traction: Get a Grip on Your Business* by Gino Wickman.

Instead of data, at that time all I had was drama. My mind

was wrestling with whether or not to pull the trigger on that deal, but what good does that do? There's nothing you can do with drama. But there's plenty of productive, profitable things you can do with data.

For example, I remember a guy I knew named Mike who ran an HVAC company. He was sending 200,000 postcards in a month. He made this substantial investment of time and money (about $100,000 worth at 50 cents per postcard). It seemed like a really ambitious and admirable investment to a lot of people. Unfortunately, the data didn't back up his decision. It might sound awesome that he sent out 200,000 postcards, but at a predicted response rate of around 1 percent, that gave them 2,000 calls to make in a month. The problem was Mike couldn't handle taking 2,000 phone calls per month, so his strategy didn't even make sense. The data indicated he would have more work than he could handle, so a good portion of his investment was wasted.

I see this sort of wastefulness all the time from ego-driven business owners. They throw big money at anything trendy or eye-catching to others, solely to show off that they've done something big. This case also proves my point that massive relentless action is BS!

Drama exists everywhere, but you can't waste your time with it. People will make excuses about their competition having deeper pockets and unfair advantages, but that's all BS. Reliable, purposeful data is the only thing that matters.

Data doesn't lie. The scoreboard in a football game will tell you who is winning and who is losing every time with no exceptions. The players and fans can argue all they want about whose team is better, who has the best athletes, who has the best uniforms, and so on. But the score of the game is the only thing that actually matters, despite all the contributing factors and pointless drama that might exist around it.

The same thing applies to the scoreboard in your industry. Who has the better product? Who has the best brand identity? Who has the coolest office?

Who cares? Check the data because that's all that matters.

While I'm relating data to a football game, I'd also like to note that if most people pay as much attention to their business data as they do to the stats of their favorite athletes, they will be hugely successful. It's actually a little mind boggling how many people can tell me the total number of yards Aaron Rodgers threw for in a given season but can't tell me the KPIs for their business...just a thought.

Don't get caught up in the drama because that's never

going to be your real problem. It's only a problem you think you have, but you really don't. When you give in to drama and try to control things beyond yourself, you lose focus and your business suffers. That can cause your business to appear to be idling or standing still because you're too busy addressing things you can't do anything about. But you're not just idling either, it's worse than that.

In business, if you're not growing, you're dying. That is another way of saying, "Do you want to be in business or not?" If you don't want to grow, then you really don't want to be in business. There is no in-between.

MARK'S MOTTO #2: "MIND YOUR OWN EFFING BUSINESS"

Another motto I live by is "Mind your own effing business."

It may sound a little crude, but I want to keep it real with you. I think it's also something I think a lot of people just pay lip service to rather than actually live by. I know I've been guilty of this same thing in the past, so I completely understand how people fall victim to worrying too much about what everybody else is doing or saying.

Whenever I catch myself in that sort of nonproductive thought pattern, I just remember, "Hey, Mark, mind your own effing business!" It's a good reality check that keeps me focused on the only thing I can control, which is me. It's easy enough to remember, and it will work for you too.

Invest your time wisely in what you do have control over. If the competition has a bigger market share, that probably means you have more time than they do. If so, you need to leverage that asset to dig deep and connect with your clients on a different level. There is a good chance that investment of time will pay off in more business from your current clients, as well as new business from outside your existing customer base. When you mind your own effing business, you correctly concentrate on ways to grow rather than foolishly think about the things you don't have at your disposal. Always remember, there's no need to waste your time counting other people's money because that takes your focus away from your money.

I see a lot of people watching what others are doing in an effort to mimic them, but they only have microinsights on what's really happening. For instance, you could find yourself at an event where everyone in the room is talking about how great this new customer relationship management (CRM) software is. Without thinking it through all the way, maybe you jump at the chance to purchase and implement it in your business. Over time, you might realize that this software just doesn't work well for your particular needs. Two years later, you could still be fighting with it and losing money due to a whole host of reasons. At that point, you need to reset and find a different system, which means you've wasted a whole lot of time and money on something because you didn't just mind your own effing business!

When you focus on what others are doing, you take your eyes off what you're doing, which is a mistake. I see a lot of great people get off track by mimicking. Instead, focus on you, your unique advantage to the world, and your data.

The media throws so much negativity at us these days. It's easy to get caught up in political agendas, soaring fuel prices, and bickering dialogue between nations. If you find yourself getting caught up by all those things that are way beyond your control, it's time to redirect your focus. Instead, I recommend refocusing your efforts on the creation of what I like to call a "Me Economy."

THE ME ECONOMY: LEVERAGING RESOURCES VERSUS RESOURCEFULNESS

There's so much noise in the world today. Everybody has a political rant they're posting on Facebook. People are concerned about how interest rates will affect the economy. Taxes aren't fair. Gas prices are going up and down and back up again. The list goes on and on, but whining about them isn't going to do anything.

So many people waste so much brain power on these external factors, but at the end of the day, none of it should hold you back. So, what if a new president is elected and you don't agree with his politics? Who cares if gas prices are up? There's nothing you can do about either one anyway. You're much better off focusing on what you can control—your Me Economy.

When you block out all the noise and focus exclusively on your own needs, you'll discover new ways to grow your business and/or change some of the things you want to change in your life and even the world around you.

The Me Economy is all about focusing on what you do best and how to make the most of it. In business and in life, you have two ways to get ahead. One way is by leveraging resources like money, power, and technology. Another is by leveraging your own resourcefulness.

When I was a kid, I was a bit shorter than most of the other kids my age, so I used my personality as my unique advantage. Maybe you're especially charming, stunningly attractive, or super intelligent. Make the most out of whatever advantage you have to separate you from the rest of the world. That's called leveraging your resourcefulness to stand out from the crowd.

BEWARE OF LAGGING INDICATORS

Whether you leverage your resources, resourcefulness, or some combination of both, it's important to realize that you have a business, not a job, and there's a big distinction to be made between those two.

In business, you need to plant seeds that will help you grow. A lot of business owners approach me with a similar problem. Hypothetically, let's say the owner of a car dealership tells me, "Mark, I'm not selling enough cars lately." On the surface, not selling enough cars looks like the real problem because it's backed up by data. In other words, if he needs to sell ten cars per month and he's only selling five, the problem is that he's five sales short per month, right?

Wrong. The data runs much deeper than that. The number of cars being sold is a lagging indicator of marketing. Deals don't just happen by themselves overnight. You need to plant seeds like marketing to make them grow. So, the real problem in that situation is in the data—the marketing numbers. It could be that there is not enough business from referrals, poorly executed email marketing campaigns, or a dozen other things. Maybe his best salesperson has been out sick for a few weeks. This point applies to any other business as well. It doesn't matter if you're selling cars, closing contracts, or anything else. You always want to find the key performance indicators

(KPI) that give you an insight most never experience. Getting the right KPIs dialed in to your business puts you at an amazing advantage because it's almost like you can predict the future.

That is such an easy mistake to make because I have done it many times as well. In the past, I have looked into how I can make more deals without realizing that to fix the real problem, I needed to find the correct KPI within the marketing budget and focus on it.

Problems like that happen all the time, and the only thing that can straighten them out is to plant the seeds that create automated, replicable processes. If you're not taking the necessary time to do that, then you have a job, not a business. You're not running a business unless there is some form of consistency involved in the processes.

One example of such a process is email marketing. That is a seed capable of growing millions of dollars in revenue with the press of a button on your computer keyboard. It takes resources to set up, but after it's established, you can repeat that process over and over again to make a lot of money while working much less. Remember, you can work smarter, not necessarily harder. If you think a process in unsustainable, ditch it and find one that's more easily replicated. Or at least find a way to automate it.

I really like email marketing to grow companies as it's easier than ever to create the proper funnel to bring prospects in, nurture them, and extract them as a client, with most of it if not all being 100 percent automated.

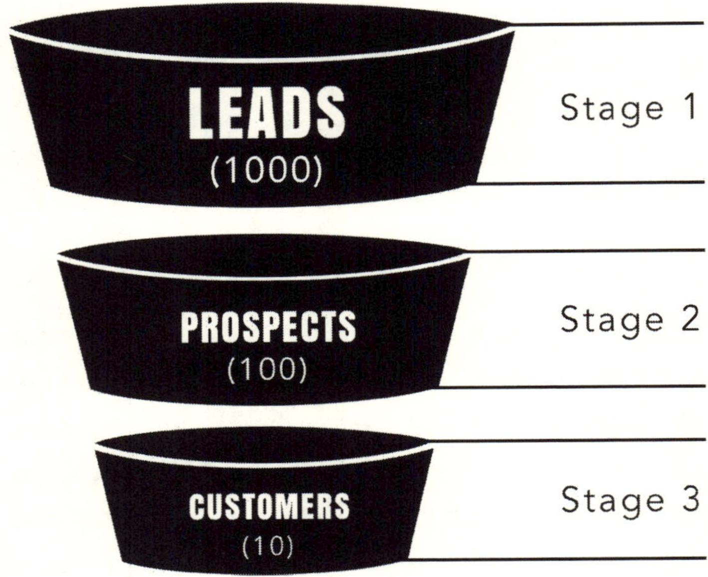

An entire book about email marketing could be written. In fact, many of them have been, and I encourage you to do some more intensive research on the subject by reading one or more of them. I've been doing email marketing for my businesses since 2005 and we're still learning and editing the path. It's a powerful, yet overlooked or underutilized approach by many business leaders.

My teams send emails five days per week. I recommend

you start with just one per week and enjoy the results. Email marketing is such an effective growth tool that you're losing out big-time if you're not implementing it on at least a small level.

If you're interested in learning more about the tremendous value and potential of email marketing as well as other great business insights, I highly recommend a book written by Russell Brunson called *Expert Secrets: The Underground Playbook for Finding Your Message, Building a Tribe, and Changing the World.*

Occasionally, the process can't save you. It's important to remember to not get too deep into marketing data exclusively because there are other indicators to consider. For example, if someone tells me, "Mark, I've sent ten thousand postcards and received zero responses," this is an indicator of a serious problem that is likely not data driven. I would start by asking that person if I could see their postcard, because there might be a serious flaw with the message. Maybe the telephone number is wrong. It sounds silly, but we've sent cards out with one digit off and mistakenly thought the marketing was bad. When we discovered the problem and fixed the number, the same campaign became a huge success.

Some other things that can go wrong could be that the contact info was too hard to find, or there could also be something off-putting about the message. Maybe the list you're going to is a market mismatch. You need to consider a depth of possible indicators when marketing campaigns perform poorly.

The lesson is to keep your mind open. Yes, the right data could easily tell you what the real problems is, but it's most crucial to consider the big picture of your business to get a clear vision of where the real problems are. One must look at the full picture of data (the macro level) and then microdata to make sure they are making decisions that can positively affect the big picture based on data. For example, consider someone selling a product online via a website.

If they get 1,000 clicks with a 50 percent opt-in rate on a web page, that's 500 opt-ins for this example. That's a very good rate, which is what many business owners strive to achieve. But if that same person uses blind copy, which says something like, "Hey, click here for a free car!" they might get 10,000 clicks with a 10 percent opt-in rate which would give them 1,000 opt-ins. That lower opt-in rate, however, would typically make much more money because there are 500 more prospects in the funnel in that situation. So that online seller might feel or appear like a loser if they're only focused on opt-in rate, but they still made more money, so what does that really mean? In this case, the opt-in rate only tells part of the story. I see many folks looking at the wrong numbers to make decisions, which is why it's important to look at the full picture.

Sometimes people get too hung up on the little things. Response rates are important, but you need to have the correct context. Annual salary is important too, but that doesn't tell the full value of a team member either. You need to see the full picture of your data, whether it's response rates, annual salary, or anything else. For example, what would you guess Tony Hsieh, the CEO of Zappos, makes in annual salary: $50 million? $25 million? Maybe $10 million? It's actually only $35,000, which is probably a lot less than many of his team members make per year.

If you're making millions of dollars while competing with a company like Zappos but only seeing what they're doing from the outside in, you might not understand the full picture of what Tony is trying to accomplish. He is much more interested in building a long-term brand while making a short-term minimal salary. His goals might be far different from your goals and vice versa.

RUN YOUR BUSINESS. DON'T PLAY IT

Another problem people think they have is believing they need a piece of paper like a license, degree, or designation that says they're qualified to do something before they actually do it. They'll say, "Mark, I want to become a real estate investor, but I have to get my license first."

"To hell with that," I say. Who needs a license? Doctors need to be licensed, not real estate investors. In fact, there are plenty of careers and businesses that require licenses, but it is important to know if it is really necessary for your particular industry. My suggestion is to use common sense and to make sure that if you are getting a certification, degree, or license, that it is for the right reason and not just to delay taking a leap into what you really want to do in life.

The only thing a license is going to do for a real estate investor is enable procrastination. It's going to make you focus on the wrong problem, which is playing business, rather than actually running a business. Kids love having a fake police badge or a fake driver's license when they want to play cops and robbers with their friends. This is the real world. Run your business, don't play it. Remember, getting a license for most part is teaching you how to pass a test, not build a business. Part of our society dictates that if you get a degree, everything will be okay, but that's not true. A degree is just a piece of paper. Of course, you could go on to do great things with a degree, but you could also do great things without one. It depends what you're trying to accomplish. Don't be degree-oriented, be success-oriented.

For most people, it's easier to move toward something like learning and test taking when it's in one's wheelhouse, but when you step into the business world, one can fail. In the world business leaders live in, I realized if you're not failing daily at something, you're not pushing enough or progressing.

For example, I know a guy who boasts about making $3 million per year without selling anything. He gets a little frustrated when I tell him he's stealing from himself and his family, because if he can make $3 million without selling anything, imagine what he could make if he did sell...$20 million, $30 million, or more? To me, this person is failing because he's only scratching the surface of what's possible for his business and for his future. If he would step it up, he'd be able to give to the world at such a different level.

Procrastination is somewhat of a natural aspect of being human. A lot of us put our dreams on hold because we're terrified of being told no. Remember, you are the creator of your own dreams and in control of your own life. You are the only one who can decide if those dreams become a reality or not. Being comfortable with and even embracing the word "no" is a big step in the right direction to growing your business and getting what you want out of life. In the next chapter, you'll discover all about finding your "no-tivation."

CHAPTER FOUR

FINDING YOUR NO-TIVATION

A rejection is nothing more than a necessary step in the pursuit of success.

—BO BENNETT, AMERICAN BUSINESSMAN AND AUTHOR

Business owners wear many hats, especially in the beginning. It's consistent with the fact that we're trying to do everything at that point. No matter what business you're in, one of those hats is going to be sales. That's why learning how to take no for an answer is a critical factor in the success of any business person.

We all know that business is a numbers game, but when a lot of people hear no, it throws them off. However, when I hear no, I don't hear rejection in a negative way. The no could mean many different things at that moment. Truth is, it's not about *us*; it's about the *client*, so I focus on the big picture goal, which is to take the emotional equation out of the picture. When one does that, they'll start to hear yes more often. My advice is to use no as power.

No in sales also means I'm one call closer to getting a yes, because I'm learning how to position my pitch better and how to listen better to the clients' questions. Occasionally, a salesperson will approach me with a distraught mentality because they've heard no thirteen times in a row, so this is like getting rejected for a date by thirteen different prospects. Anytime somebody comes to me with such a problem, my answer is, "Okay, well, go get told no a hundred times more now." Not only do I give people permission to take no for an answer, but I encourage it because it takes the stress out of the process. "Remember," I'll explain to them, "you're not the one getting rejected. It's the process or product."

That's where "data, not drama" takes over again. Sure, some people are better at sales than others, but it's more about process and product than anything else. I never need to awkwardly tell somebody, "Look, I'm afraid you just suck at sales." Instead, if a salesperson has a quota of $100,000 for a quarter, but they only hit $50,000, I can start by asking them how many calls they made. Then, I can ask them if they can double the number of calls necessary to reach their quota. If they can't, then we both know they can't do the job. That's okay, but the data shows both of us that the process isn't right for them.

To find your no-tivation, start by learning not to take no personally or to think it's a permanent answer. Then, understand that abundant opportunities remain. On your next attempt, change your approach, or maybe find a new presentation format. There could be many different things that your no-tivation will uncover that turn your next attempt into a done deal and ongoing increased success.

Of course, finding your no-tivation is about more than just sales.

WHEN YOU HEAR NO, DON'T GET FRUSTRATED; GET DETERMINED

I officially began my life as a remote business owner on December 31, 2005. I remember sitting at a roundtable in Columbus, Ohio, with my team, discussing how the company was going to be run from that day forward.

"Hey everybody," I began. "I'm leaving for about a month, and I'm counting on all of you to step up in a big way."

That opening statement caused some initial murmurs around the table, as well as some confusion and momentary chaos.

When the dust settled a bit, I continued, "Trust me, I know you can do this. From now on, we're going to close deals without me being present and send money remotely via wire transfer. Actually, we're going to work remotely as much as possible. We don't need to meet to discuss every little detail of each transaction. If somebody wants to see a deal, they can figure out how to make that happen. You're all very capable of making this work. I believe deeply in all of you. Any questions?"

A lot of people responded immediately by voicing their displeasure for the situation. "No way, Mark," they said. "There is no way that can ever work. You're insane...just... No!"

It's funny, but the more I heard no that day, the more I became convinced that I could pull it off. Most people seem prewired to avoid no and seek yes, but not me. Maybe that says something about how my psychological profile might occasionally stray from the norm, but that day I learned how to turn no into something pretty damned great. The birth of the virtualization of my business began because I found my no-tivation, and I made it work.

VIRTUALIZATION IS REALITY

My business—real estate investing—was a very hands-on business many years ago. Closing a real estate deal meant all the stakeholders getting together at the title company or a lawyer's office to sign paperwork, close the deal, and bring in the bank checks for the necessary funds. It was such a lengthy process, which was fine when technology didn't exist to make it much quicker and easier. The more I thought about it, the more I realized how unnecessary the whole process had become. This wasn't unique to real estate either. Most businesses were moving to a new reality of virtualization.

I knew I needed to find a way to refine the traditional process of making real estate deals. First, I had to find someone on my team who could act as my representative at the closing. That process is even easier today through electronic signature or a mobile notary.

Second, I needed to find a way to transfer the money electronically. That process is also exponentially easier today, but in those days, my bank didn't have a way of electronically transferring the money from a computer. You had to go to the bank and get a check and fill out all the paperwork. I found a workaround by hiring an extremely tech-savvy professional who was highly skilled at setting up wire transfers. Today, you can wire money from your phone in about twelve seconds or less. In short, virtualization is reality today; back then, it wasn't, but I made it happen because I wasn't satisfied settling for the status quo. I sought solutions, not problems.

By finding someone to represent me at closings and hiring a professional to set up wire transfers, I streamlined two time-consuming and inefficient processes in my business. It enabled me to close a deal and have money transferred to the proper accounts from anywhere in the world. A couple key results occurred from this new-and-improved business model.

First, I haven't been to a property we've purchased since 2005, which has freed up my time to make much more money and enjoy life on a much deeper level. It's kind of what this book is all about. Also, although most of our deals are still in Ohio today, my entire team is now based in Palm Beach, Florida, and the business is flourishing more than it ever did when everybody was in Ohio. Long story, short—the results have been awesome!

Why waste your time traveling to a sterile office environment in Poughkeepsie, New York, or Muncie, Indiana, to close a deal when you can skip all the BS and get business done with a press of the Return button on your computer keyboard from a posh island resort instead? Virtualization is the way a lot of businesses are run today. Real estate is only one of a countless number of industries that operate on a server these days, instead of an office space.

When people tell you no, it's important to think deeply about what they're actually saying no to. When I hear no,

I don't hear anything like, "No, and don't ever call me back," or, "No, you suck." I hear something more like, "No, not right now."

A lot of people might think salespeople are generally bulletproof, but my experience tells me that most salespeople are highly susceptible to the fear of rejection because they think everything is about them all the time. I get it because that used to be exactly how I felt too. Fortunately, a mentor of mine turned that around for me many years ago when he told me, "Guess what, Mark? It's not all about you."

That somewhat humbling but important realization, along with the fact that I love consultative selling but detest the traditional hardcore approach to sales, enabled me to approach no from a different perspective. Now, when I hear no, I don't take it personally for a couple reasons. First, I realize it's not me that the person is saying no to. Second, I also understand that I'm planting a seed for a potentially different outcome in the future.

Note: If you're interested in learning more about the fine art of consultative selling, check out anything written by Jeffrey Gitomer. *The Little Red Book of Selling* is an especially good read.

AN ABUNDANCE MINDSET

Closely related to finding your no-tivation is the importance of keeping an abundance mindset. It extends to every aspect of your life. The abundance mindset also works hand in hand with the idea of leveling-up in Chapter Two, where I mentioned buying nicer jeans and going to great restaurants. Now, I'd like to share with you how this really took a turn for me in a positive way by flying first class.

By not flying first class, I was unknowingly placing limitations on my mindset. The nice jeans looked and felt great, but they were somewhat of a contradiction when I walked into my cramped coach seat every time I flew.

When I started flying first class, I realized that I was transforming my thinking. It allowed me to adopt the practices and mindset of the most successful people in the world. That's exactly where I needed to be, and it's where you need to be too.

The first few times, I struggled to pay for the first-class airfare mentally, but it really opened up my mind to the abundance mindset. Limitations are for losers. Flying first class was probably the best way for me to fully understand and reap the rewards of the abundance mindset. In the beginning, I felt like I was wasting money and stealing from myself, but I realized that wasn't true at all. The only thing that really changed was my mindset.

Still not convinced you should stop flying coach and go first class?

Think of it this way: Do you still drive the first car you owned? What about the first apartment you lived in?

Those items still exist, but at this stage of your life and success, you probably wouldn't be caught dead in either one. The only thing that has changed is your mindset, and that's a good thing. Going from coach to first class is no different than going from that beat-up, old car with 200,000 miles on it or that run-down, old apartment you shared with three roommates to what you're in now. And as you work this mindset muscle for the rest of your life, you'll realize that levels upon more levels start opening up.

As one of my mentors would say, *"Select excellence over adequacy!"*

FROM SEVENTY-SIX DOLLARS OF DESPERATION TO SUCCESS

Having an abundance mindset is much more than just looking like success. It can often mean the difference between going broke and achieving booming success. Consider the following story about a follower of mine who serves as a great example of that.

This business owner reached out not too long ago and

confided to me, "Hey Mark, I'm in real trouble. I've got seventy-six dollars left in my bank account, and my confidence is completely shot. In fact, I'm scared shitless because my wife doesn't even realize we have no money left."

I replied, "Okay, just try to relax for a minute, and we'll figure this out together. Tell me, what's the data look like?" That was my way of taking emotion out of the situation. At that point, we were talking about hard facts—numbers—to determine the problem. It wasn't about him that way; it was about the data. Then, he laid everything out for me. As he was talking, it became abundantly clear that desperation had taken over his entire approach. He probably ran into a few too many no responses in a row for his own comfort level (aka ego) and started to panic. He lost control.

Then, I asked him, "Do you want me to shoot straight with you or sugarcoat this?"

He told me, "Be honest Mark, I need some help."

I said, "Hey, what the hell are you doing? You're a smart guy. You're not supposed to be doing shit like that. Right now, you're doing everything wrong, and that's not you. You're going after the wrong people. You're having the wrong conversations. You're not value adding them.

You're desperate right now, and desperation never makes a decent sale, never!"

As I explained all that, it seemed like it all rang very true to him. He realized that he knew better than to just take a shotgun approach to sales. His process suffered severely because he allowed a few too many no responses to shake his confidence and subsequently alter his approach in a very negative way. We talked a little more about what he was doing wrong and how he could potentially fix it. There were a lot of ideas thrown around, but it really came down to him just starting to get focused on what was important and do the work. Desperation and his ego were getting the best of him.

Shortly after our conversation, I got a couple texts from him.

The first one read, "Just made a $5,600 sale!"

Then, "There goes another $7,000!"

Thankfully, the beat went on for him, and I shot him back a text. "Congratulations! Now, stop texting me every time you make an effing sale...lol."

In seemingly no time at all, he was back to selling like a rock star, which doesn't surprise me at all because he was always a very smart, talented guy. He just needed an emotional reset.

In the next chapter, we'll take a deep dive into focused action. Just like my friend needed to stop taking a shotgun approach to sales and focus his efforts on the right conversations with the right people, you'll need to know how to go all in on your strengths while properly addressing your weaknesses as well. We all have amazing abundant opportunity if we're paying attention to it!

CHAPTER FIVE

WHY SUMO WRESTLERS MAKE LOUSY SOCCER PLAYERS

There is only one corner of the universe you can be certain of improving, and that's your own self.

—ALDOUS HUXLEY, ENGLISH NOVELIST AND PHILOSOPHER

They call me the Deal Maker or DM for short. It's a nickname my lifelong friend Bill gave me when I was about nineteen years old. I've known Bill my whole life, and he's more like a brother to me than just another friend. He's the one who first called me the Deal Maker because I was in the habit of making deals everywhere we went.

Bill and I were working construction jobs at the time. Strangely enough, I never thought of my deal-making the same way he did. In my mind, I was there to serve more than I was to make money. I was just listening, gaining knowledge, enhancing my skills, and putting deals together. It felt like something I was supposed to do. But Bill would always observe with some amazement and say something like, "Dude, do you not see what you're doing? Guys are constantly hiring you to work for them. You're making a shitload of money!"

I was the winning bidder on construction projects quite often that were worth tens of thousands of dollars, sometimes even upwards of $100,000. I would pull up to the site in a beat-up, old pickup truck while the other contractors would pull up in luxury sedans or sports cars, and it amazed Bill often that my bid beat their bid, which happened with a fair amount of regularity.

That's not the way I saw it though. I knew I was making a lot of money for a dopey eighteen-year-old kid who almost didn't graduate high school, but I wasn't really surprised by these guys hiring me so often. I thought, "Why wouldn't they hire me?" I was good at construction because I had been doing it with my dad since I was ten years old. Actually, we both knew I was good at construction. We also both knew that I was not so great at the administrative side of the business. In fact, Bill agreed that I sucked at paperwork. It was definitely a weakness which I've since realized is a common weakness for business leaders.

FOCUS ON YOUR STRENGTHS, HIRE YOUR WEAKNESSES

Sumo wrestlers are great at sumo wrestling. Big surprise, I know. But how good do you think they would be at soccer? Just picture a 400-pound man wearing a precariously placed loincloth and gasping for air while clutching his chest as he tries to chase down a comparatively tiny checkered ball in the middle of an enormous grassy field. Obviously, that wouldn't work out very well. In fact, the paramedics would likely be called to duty in a matter of minutes. For an even more extreme example, picture that same sumo wrestler as a jockey at the Kentucky Derby. I'm guessing the American Society for the Prevention of Cruelty to Animals would have to get involved in that situation.

There's a reason 400-pound men don't play soccer. They're not good at it, so they focus on what they are good at, like grappling with another 400-pound man and trying to throw him outside a marked circle to win the undying respect, honor, and eternal adoration of his entire country.

I sucked at paperwork. In fact, a sumo wrestler may have a better shot at scoring a goal in the World Cup than I did at accurately filling out paperwork in a timely manner, so I stopped doing it.

That's when I decided to hire my way out of my weaknesses. I simply hired someone to do the paperwork for me. First of all, I hated doing paperwork. It was like poison to me. Secondly, the person I hired to do it was a hell of a lot better at it than I was.

Invoicing was one area of paperwork that really needed someone else's skillset. I was great at making money but terrible at collecting it because I was too damned busy thinking about my next project to collect on the current one. A lot of us fall into that trap. You need to make sure someone collects the money for your hard work, and if you're as bad as I am at doing it, hire it out!

The true beauty of that solution is that not being forced to take up so much valuable time with paperwork gave me the freedom to close more deals and make more money. It gave me a refined focus and allowed me to address a weakness that was holding me back. More than that, it changed my whole business, which subsequently changed my life.

Everybody has weaknesses. Don't ignore them because that mentality isn't going to solve any problems. You need to acknowledge your weaknesses and hire people who have a strength in that area. Honestly, you might even consider hiring out some of your strengths too. For instance, I am great at selling and deal-making, but I eventually hired it out anyway because it wasn't the best use of my time. I can make much more money if I reallocate the time I spend making deals to more big-picture thinking. The lesson is, don't hold on to some tasks just because you're great at them. Make sure the tasks you hold on to are also the best uses of your time.

Identifying strengths and weaknesses not only in yourself but in everyone around you is one thing that will enable you to assemble a team of top contributors. Instead of asking, "How do I build an amazing team?" The better question is, "How do I focus on what I'm great at and put other people in place to do what I suck at?"

Putting your team members in the best position to succeed doesn't stop at the hiring process. One day you may discover that your assistant has some kickass marketing skills. Maybe it's an untapped skill that went unnoticed by all previous employers. If you're correctly focused on your strengths as a leader, the strengths of those around you will become obvious, and you'll be able to make some shifts on your team that will enhance productivity across the board. After all, even a sumo wrestler is capable of dropping a few hundred pounds, and from there, maybe he could become a decent midfielder.

In the next chapter, I will explain how business leaders can fall into a trap called FOMO, which stands for the Fear of Missing Out. It's a similar concept to why a sumo wrestler makes for a lousy soccer player. When business leaders experience FOMO, they mistakenly focus their efforts on a trending business, technology, or marketing tactic they're not ideally suited for solely because they don't want to be left behind the times. Keep reading to learn more about how I've fallen victim to this trap and why you should avoid making the same mistake.

CHAPTER SIX

USING POWER FOCUS TO GROW YOUR BUSINESS

Lack of direction, not lack of time is the problem. We all have twenty-four hour days.

—ZIG ZIGLAR, AMERICAN AUTHOR AND MOTIVATIONAL SPEAKER

Years ago, I hired someone to run a cold-calling operation for my business. We had about twelve reps (maybe more) in Florida making hundreds of cold calls per day. It was an intense atmosphere, but it wasn't results-driven enough for me. I'm much better off in a hustle-bustle business model with a little more direct control over the results.

That business model was concerned too much with lead stress. We needed a ridiculously high number of leads per rep to make that work, and as a result, our budget went through the roof. There was almost no control over how successful the business was going to be from month to month, and that wasn't a good fit for my methodology. Eventually, I realized that particular business wasn't right for me and I stepped away. It was taking too much of my focus away from what our team was great at.

A lot of other business owners make the same mistake of trying to create something they're not great at. There's a fear-of-missing-out (FOMO) mindset that is fairly prevalent in today's business environment. People are afraid that if they don't broaden their horizons, they might miss out on the next great money-making opportunity. The truth, however, is that it's much more important to "power focus" on what you're great at than risk venturing into something you *might* be good at but not great. Furthermore, if 80 percent of your money is coming from 20 percent of your business, just imagine the growth that can take place if you focus 100 percent of your efforts on that 20 percent of your business that is making more than three-quarters of your money. Therefore, does it make sense to spread yourself out over additional areas of stress that likely won't make much money? Or does it sound smarter to ditch those other things and focus your efforts?

As a businessperson, it's easy to fall into Shiny Object Syndrome. When business gets boring, a lot of people feel the need to unnecessarily shake things up and stray from what they do best. But business isn't meant to be fun, exciting, or crazy in any way. Actually, it's meant to be just the opposite. In fact, I grew my company by focusing on the boring and hiring folks to do the boring things. This is easier said than done, but I can tell you that this piece—if you get it—can change your business life in a big way. Remember, what's boring to a business owner is very comforting to some folks. It took me years to realize that, but thanks to the book mentioned below, it's much easier to identify your Unique Ability®.

There's a great book called *Unique Ability 2.0* by Catherine Nomura, Julia Waller, and Shannon Waller. This book greatly helped me to dial in to the concept of my Unique Ability and significantly grow my business. It's based on a concept by Dan Sullivan and does a great job of explaining how to align what you're doing properly with where you want to go, what you're trying to do and what you're best at. I recommend reading it for a much deeper discussion about growing your business through power focus.

GO DEEPER, NOT WIDER

Following the same mindset, one great marketing strategy is much more valuable than one hundred mediocre strategies. Facebook, Craigslist, YouTube, Instagram, email, direct mail, television, and radio, among many others, are all perfectly acceptable choices for the allocation of marketing dollars. I suggest, however, going deeper with one of them rather than wider by spending a little on each of them. The real question is, which one should you power focus on?

The answer to that depends on a few factors. For instance, you might be amazing at television advertising and infomercials. Maybe you've got an all-American appearance that people react extraordinarily well to. You might also have an effective way of delivering a message with your voice, but perhaps you suck at writing and social messaging, like I suck at paperwork. If all those things are true, it doesn't make sense to waste any of your valuable time or financial resources on anything other than interpersonal communication via electronic media. Therefore, get your All-American good looks on television and your golden pipes on the radio as much as possible.

Of course, just the opposite could be true. You could be a regular Bill Shakespeare with the written word, but maybe you're not quite as gifted visually or audibly. In that case, it makes sense to stay away from television and radio while committing a power focus to written marketing campaigns.

The one great marketing strategy you choose depends largely on your individual skillset, as well as your particular budget and the number of leads required to be successful. Some people need fewer high-quality leads, while others need a larger quantity of less expensive leads. It all depends on your business model. The broader lesson here is to discover what your particular needs are and go deeper with one great strategy while eliminating the one hundred or more other possibilities that aren't as good.

It is also important to ignore what works for other people. This gets back to Mark's Motto #2, which is, "Mind your own effing business." For instance, some people thought what we were doing in that cold-calling business was awesome. They saw hundreds of thousands of leads coming in and mistakenly thought we were positively killing it and started to mimic us. The truth was we weren't killing anything except ourselves and our money. The people who thought we were would have been much better off focusing on finding their own best marketing strategy instead of envying our misguided steps.

The biggest reason I urge you to go deep with marketing, not wide, is because it's close to impossible to be great at more than one or two channels. For example, I like direct mail—even today with all the other online sources—as it has a number of variables to explore. It's impossible to extract something from all of them while also trying to effectively push Facebook or Instagram campaigns because there just isn't enough time to do them all effectively, unless you have a team of folks that are great at each piece.

When leaders start paying too much attention to what everybody else is doing, they inevitably get sidetracked and fall victim to FOMO. They start dabbling in all these other outlets, and things can go awry very quickly from there. It's happened to me before, but the most impactful situation I can remember was with a business owner named Tom who approached me a few years ago.

Tom explained to me, "I'm all over the place with marketing, and things are spiraling out of control all of a sudden. There is a bunch of really cool stuff I'm involved with, but none of it is working right now, and I have to make some changes. I have to let some people go, and I hate doing that. I feel like I'm losing control, and I need to get things right again."

The first mistake Tom made was in his perception that he was working for himself. It was all about what he was pioneering, rather than helping his team to succeed. I always look at my role as if I'm working for others. If I get sidetracked and fail at something, the people around me go away because I won't be able to afford to pay them anymore. In that sense, I work for them. It's my job to give them the tools, leads, and opportunities to succeed, which, ultimately, helps me to succeed.

Tom also made the mistake of getting sidetracked. He lost his focus on what was working for him, and it had dire consequences. After he explained to me what was happening, I asked him a really simple question: "Well, what did you do in the past that worked?"

He replied, "Nothing revolutionary or terribly exciting. I used direct mail."

"Okay, that sounds like a good idea. How much are you investing in direct mail now?" I asked.

"About 20 percent of my marketing budget," he said.

I paused just to see if the answer would come to him, but it didn't right away. It seemed obvious to me that if he was only allocating 20 percent to direct mail, which worked well in the past, he needed to go deeper into it, so I responded, "This isn't that hard Tom. You need to allocate 100 percent of your marketing budget to direct mail. I know it's not exciting, but do you want to be exciting or successful?"

Sometimes we don't see the answer that is right in front of us, which is what happened to Tom in that situation. He spent so much time and energy on the latest and greatest that he stepped away from what he was truly great at—direct mail. After I explained my boring but potentially valuable recommendation, he went into freak-out mode for a few minutes, "But I spent so much effing time and money on those things!"

"Who cares," I replied. "Those things aren't working. Get back to what does work for you. You're obviously great at direct mail, so stick with it."

Tom agreed and went all in on the marketing tactic he was great at. It took about three months for the data to catch up, but when it did, it caught up so well that his business has been booming ever since. In fact, he has even hired back a lot of the people he had to let go when he briefly lost his focus, and now he is having record-breaking months. More importantly, he has gained his time and freedom back.

Find out what you're great at and stick with it because that will be your most direct path to exponential growth. One of my companies has been implementing the same marketing channel—direct mail—for nearly twenty-two years now, and it is still working great and providing growth, but my media company is 100 percent online through email marketing, so I am living proof that either approach can work. I've invested millions of dollars in both, but the question is, which one will work for you? Maybe both.

Millennials may find the direct-mail approach especially odd because their generation is more comfortable with technology and social media than anything else. My real estate company, however, has been buying houses from direct mail every month, and our business has never been better. That doesn't mean it's going to work for you in your business, but just make sure you don't underestimate the ability of the tried-and-true marketing strategies.

Direct mail will probably work forever. A lot of people think technology is killing it, but that isn't true. In fact, the better technology gets, the more effective direct mail becomes because less people are doing it, and we have the long-term data on our side to validate that statement.

Remember, *data, not drama.*

FOMO kicks in easily for people who see a flashy new technology. They don't want to be the ones still using a desk Rolodex full of business cards when everybody else has their contacts digitally loaded into their smartphone, so they jump on something like Facebook ads, without considering if it aligns well with what their company is and what they're trying to do as a business owner. That's not meant to disparage social media though, because it is extremely effective for some businesses. It's very data-rich and allows you to track and analyze almost anything. The point is to find out which marketing tactic aligns best with your strengths as a leader and the business you're running and stick with it, whether it's direct mail, social media, or giant fuzzy mascots wearing an advertisement board around their necks (not likely, but you never know).

Remember, if you add another platform, you're adding complexity, which is always a difficult prospect. Know your objectives and KPIs first. Once you have a good handle on them and you see another platform that may work, do some research. If the data looks good on the new platform, maybe then give it a shot. Better yet, if you've got something that's working, stick with it or hire the proper professional to manage and deploy.

"BUSYNESS" IS NOT THE SAME THING AS "BUSINESS"

Going deep should be taken to other aspects of your business as well. It is not a strategy that is exclusive to marketing. A good example of this is the story of a business friend I met at a mastermind who had a $25-million-dollar-per-year roofing business. His story shows how important it is for business owners to not confuse "busyness" with "business."

Stress had been building in my friend for a while because he was simply doing too much. Between the new roof installations and his repair work, there was almost no time for him to unwind and enjoy his life. Finally, he had enough one day, and he took some time to figure out how he could reduce his stress. That's when he uncovered one vitally important KPI, which was that 80 percent of his profits came from his repair work.

He was only keeping around $700,000 net per year after

all the dust settled, which may sound like a lot of money, but it was not in his situation. That money could get eaten up in one bad month for him because his marketing budget was over a million per month and that didn't include the debt from all the trucks on the road and the staff required to man it up. He was only one month away at any given time from getting into serious financial trouble.

After realizing that nearly all of his net profits came from repair work, he also realized he could cut his staff down by 95 percent if he completely shut down the roof installation part of his business and only worked on repair and maintenance jobs.

In this case, my friend only needed to know one KPI, which was where most of his profits were coming from. The problem for most people is they make it more complicated than it needs to be. When a lot of business owners have a problem, they think it's a combination of seventy-five different factors, and usually it's seven or less.

Today, Mike is enjoying a much better quality of life. He makes more money than he ever did before by millions. He has more time, and he's free to divide that time however he sees fit between family, friends, and business.

At the end of the day, what does $25 million in business even mean if we're only keeping a small fraction of it. The goal of running a business isn't what we make but what we keep, right? I see this sort of thing all the time. People share big numbers that don't necessarily mean much. The real number all business owners need to focus on is *net profit*. Today, Mike is doing around $4 million and keeping over 40 percent of the profits with much less risk and significantly fewer headaches. Those numbers are much more critical than what could be seen as a gaudy $25 million in revenue.

ONLY THREE WAYS TO INCREASE REVENUE

No matter how big your numbers are or how well you're running your business, there are really only three ways to increase revenue.

1. **Increase the number of customers you serve.** Ask yourself, "How can I turn more prospects into customers? How can I create a referral program?"
2. **Increase the transactional value of a customer.** You can earn more money from a customer when you increase their value. Maybe you add a monthly program to the purchase or cross-sell them a compatible service that enhances what you're currently selling them. This will increase your transactional value and reduce the scope of your marketing costs.
3. **Increase the frequency of purchase for a customer.** There are a lot of ways to do this, including email mar-

keting, up-selling, cross-selling, or any combination of them. Ask yourself, "How can I increase each of these strategies by 10 percent in order to drive the continual growth of my business?"

Go deep, not wide with your business. Stick with what works and know the difference between busyness and business. In the next chapter, we will dig deeper into leveraging other people's time and talent. It's time to discuss how to hire, empower, and manage A-list talent.

CHAPTER SEVEN

HOW AND WHEN TO HIRE PEOPLE

An empowered organization is one in which individuals have the knowledge, skill, desire, and opportunity to personally succeed in a way that leads to collective organizational success.

—STEPHEN COVEY, AMERICAN BUSINESSPERSON, AUTHOR, AND KEYNOTE SPEAKER

I was twelve years old in 1990, making ten dollars for each lawn that I mowed in my neighborhood. To a twelve-year-old boy, ten dollars could buy a lot of baseball cards and other things, like a skateboard if I saved up enough for it. It was a pretty good deal for me at the time, but I was limiting my success because I only had so much time to mow lawns.

School took up more than half of my waking hours, and then homework took up even more time, when and if I did it. Plenty of people asked if I could add them to my list of lawns. After all, what homeowner wants to come home to mow their lawn after working ten to twelve hours a day, battling commuter traffic, and getting yelled at by their boss? They could have hired a landscaping service, but I guarantee that would have cost a lot more than ten dollars per mow. My problem was I didn't have enough time to add anyone else to my list, so I began to brainstorm.

I guess I knew at a pretty early age how valuable time was. I began to wonder, "What if I outsourced some of the lawns by paying other kids to work for me?" We could split the money from the lawns they do, and I could double or triple the money I made without having to invest any more time. Just like that, my entrepreneurial spirit took flight.

I hired some buddies I knew I could trust to do the job well, and it worked out great for all of us. My time was freed up to find more lawns, and my buddies made money without having to go out and ask people to do the work.

Oddly enough, some people had a weird way of looking at that arrangement. They said I was lazy for not doing all the work myself. I looked at it in a completely different way. I figured I was making more money than I ever would if I had to do everything myself, and besides, everyone else got what they wanted out of it too, so how was that lazy? In other words, I knew I was onto something.

Back when I was a kid, the word "entrepreneur" was synonymous with "lazy." It's different today. Entrepreneurs are seen as changing the world with creativity and innovation, but back in 1990, it meant you were too lazy to do any real work but still wanted to make a lot of money.

The truth is that I was never afraid to work hard, but I didn't want to work hard without big results to show for it. I don't think I'm any different from most other business owners in that aspect. Most of us aren't afraid of working hard, but we're all dreamers in our hearts. We envision our hard work paying off someday in a big way. The problem is that over time the vision gets muddled because we try to do everything ourselves.

The reason most business owners are afraid to hire people to help them is almost never money, although that's what most of us believe. It's actually because they always think nobody can do the work as well as they can. There are several problems with that somewhat narcissistic method of thinking, however.

First of all, they may actually do it better than you because if you're hiring correctly, you're hiring people who are great at the things you suck at most. Secondly, even if they're not as good as you at whatever you're hiring them for, they're still going to do it in a timely manner, be consistent with it, and completely take it off your to-do list, which enables you to go make more money instead of doing payroll, finding an office cleaner, or some other administrative task.

DOCUMENT EVERYTHING

Another problem many business owners have with letting go of administrative work is that they don't have any idea of how to formalize the handoff. You might be thinking that it will take you just as long or longer to explain how to do the work and actually get it done as it would if you just did it yourself. That may be true in the beginning, but once you empower your staff with the knowledge they need to implement a replicable process, it will save you a tremendous amount of time every day for the rest of your life. The key to making that happen is by first documenting your entire process, and it doesn't take elaborate PowerPoint slide decks and detailed personal presentations to do it. The key is to document, not to create.

One simple way to document everything is to pay a person twenty dollars an hour to sit in front of you, observe everything you do, and write it down or record it. You can also record your own computer screen while you work on the tasks you're looking to hand off. Speak out loud about what you're doing and record it. Then send it to a transcription service to have it documented.

My team does almost everything by recording their screen and talking about their process. It might sound something like this: "Hey guys. I'm on this website and clicking on 555 Makebelieve Street in Nonametown, Ohio. When I click the address, this is what I see." Then, we take that recording, send it to a transcription service, and they create an amazing visual process for us to use as a reference guide whenever we need it.

WHEN TO HIRE

It's time to hire someone anytime a particular action or series of actions are making you feel stressed out or overwhelmed. A good start to this process is to make a list of routine tasks that need to be executed on a regular basis, like getting the mail, ordering supplies, organizing your calendar, pushing out the email marketing, billing, creating documents, collecting, ordering, accounting, and others. In fact, there's no time like the present.

The next page is left intentionally blank. It's meant for you to write down some of your most routine tasks that you either hate doing or suck at doing. Take a decent amount of time to do it. In fact, it might be a good idea to complete a full workweek before you're done. By then, you should know that your list is comprehensive enough. When you're sure you have a complete list, hire the people who can help the most with those tasks.

No person will make a great business who wants to do it all himself or get all the credit.

—ANDREW CARNEGIE, AMERICAN INDUSTRIALIST

www.10MinuteBusinessOwner.com

SAMPLE FUN JOB ADVERTISEMENT

If you don't already have an administrative professional, it's likely that the exercise of writing down a list of routine tasks you either suck at or just hate doing has made it clear that you need to hire someone to take those things off your plate.

I've placed plenty of traditional job ads over the years, but they brought in too many people who weren't the precise cultural fit we were looking for. Once I switched to this sample of a fun job ad, it became much easier to pull in a better fit for the company. Feel free to model your own job ad after this if you like it, or just grab whatever takeaways you can from it.

Admin. Asst.—High energy, Fun Position, West Palm Beach (WPB) area

Amazing job with *very* specific requirements

Personal Assistant needed for a real estate investor based in WPB

Here is what's specifically needed from you:

1. You *must* be a self-starter. This is a small organization that does a *great* deal of business. There are *awesome* systems in place, but you'll be figuring a bit out on your own too.

2. You *need* to be *totally* comfortable with simple internet-based programs. Familiarity with Google (even Google Apps), online databases, simple html editing of pages, etc. Also, should have an above average grasp of social media. (Facebook, Twitter, and the like—If applying, *please* know what these are.)
3. Be *free* to travel about one weekend every two to three months. (We do training in some pretty cool places, but before you think it's all glam-glam, remember, there's a lot of "stuff" to be done. But hey, it's better doing "stuff" in Costa Rica or Hawaii than WPB, right?)
4. Be *comfortable* doing a small amount of personal assisting since you'll be working *directly* with me. Sometimes I will need a few errands run, such as picking up dry cleaning, dropping off FedEx packages, arranging for the housekeeper to come by, etc.

Okay, the *cool* thing is that this is a pretty laid-back job, where you get to interact with a lot of cool people. Sometimes, however, there are *deadlines and crunches* that will make the schedule more intense.

Just to set your expectations correctly, the last time I posted a job here, I received over 300 applications and called *two* people back. I hired one of them immediately, so I will *not* be responding to all applications.

Here is what I'm looking for: [See, this really *can* be easy!]

1. Tell me how you will fit in *this* job! I've laid out the job requirements as clearly as I can. I know what I'm looking for and have made them a fit. I will *not* be calling you to clarify whether or not you're a fit, so there's no second chance. Your response *is* your impression!
2. Tell me your income expectations (or range). We'll be working together, and I will be providing *very* specific communications in the future. Being vague in this area just sets up a concern that you're not going to be able to ask for what you really want later if you come on board.
3. Describe your ideal working environment—hours, flexibility or structure, casual or formal. I'm kind of open to a number of options and inflexible in a few other areas, but I want to know what works for you. I'm looking for the *ideal* fit. I don't want to go through a bunch of *trial* runs.
4. I'm glad to see your resume, but without an accompanying document (letter, rant, attachment, etc.) addressing the above, I can assure you that it will be a waste of your time.

If you've read this far...brave soul!

Congratulations because you're possibly a fit for this pretty cool job. I love what I do, and I'm looking for *one* person to help manage things going forward. I'm much tamer than I sound, but I do have very specific requirements which I communicate clearly. Then I empower you with the authority to be the enforcer!

Get those responses over as soon as you can so the *right* one of you can start working right away. Reply to the email address at the top of this listing!

Thanks!

CHAPTER EIGHT

MANAGING AND EMPOWERING PEOPLE

Your assets are your employees. Invest more on those performing well. Let the non-performers go.

—MANOJ ARORA, INDIAN SELF-HELP AUTHOR

If you haven't already done so, the first hire most people make is usually an assistant. Most of your business will flow through your assistant at some point. Typically, most business owners (myself included) suck at the paperwork, which is where an assistant will excel, especially in terms of consistency.

Patience is the key when hiring an assistant. This concept is hugely important. Understand where you came from. Remember the many times you failed when you were setting up your business or even the many businesses you failed at before this one finally took off. The same thing happens with the people you hire. You can't expect them to show up one day and inherently understand every detail of your business. They're not going to automatically make everything run like a well-oiled machine as soon as they put their lunch in the break-room refrigerator. It takes patience on your part to realize they're going to screw a few things up in the beginning, but if you stay the course and they're the right person for the job, they will eventually change your life. They'll free up your time to make much more money.

Be straight-up with a new administrative professional. Start by telling them what you need help with the most. If it's organizing your files and billing statements, tell them, "Okay, I really need some big-time help with organizing my files and billing. It's a complete mess, and it's going to be a lot of work, but it will go smoothly once we get it dialed in. Are you up for the challenge?" There's no need to fake anything. After all, there's a reason you hired someone to do something. Those routine tasks are obviously not dialed in right now, but that's why you're bringing this person in.

Start by handing them a job description with their role and responsibilities. Be reasonable about the expectations you write down and list eight to ten routine tasks that need to be duplicated every day. They don't need to be complicated. They could be getting the mail, inputting data, updating the calendar. Remember, this is just a start. Eventually, they're going to take on much more than what is on your initial list.

Anytime one of my new-hires didn't work out, it was because I didn't set them up to succeed—I actually set them up to fail without realizing it. I didn't have a job description ready for them, so they weren't able to properly identify what they were supposed to do. It's almost impossible for someone to succeed when expectations are not clearly laid out. I learned from those mistakes, however, and now, I'm sure to take the necessary time to develop real roles and responsibilities before I hire anybody. You should do the same because you need to know what you're trying to accomplish with every new-hire you make.

Evaluate their performance after the first thirty days or so, then at sixty, and again at ninety. Take as much emotion out of the process as possible and be real with them about their performance based off the data.

Once you see those eight to ten tasks performed up to or beyond your expectations every day, you can start to work with them on some of the more intricate details of how they can contribute even more. By the sheer nature of being around for a year or two, they should start to take on more responsibilities. If they have it in them, their A-list talent will start to shine when they get comfortable.

HIRE FAST—FIRE FAST!

A popular mantra of business owners today is "Hire slow—fire fast!" Unfortunately, most of us do the opposite. Often times, we're so excited about the idea of taking some routine tasks off our plate that we hire the first person with a decent resume who shows up on time for their interview.

Before you pull the trigger on hiring anybody for your business, you need to know precisely where you need help. Otherwise, you'll end up wasting resources by hiring someone who is either unqualified or unneeded. That doesn't help you, nor does it help the person you hire.

Hiring fast is fine as long as you are well-prepared to hire the right person for the right job. But you should also fire fast because if you think you need to let somebody go, they probably think the same thing. Therefore, I prefer the hiring mantra of "Hire fast—fire fast!"

I'm an emotional person, so I'm just as guilty of delaying the occasionally inevitable and unenviable task of firing a team member. I try as hard as I can to be quick about it, but the truth is that I like my people a lot, and my emotions get in the way sometimes. That is why earlier, I mentioned using data to keep team members or let them go. It takes the emotion out of the equation as much as possible.

Although the staff member usually knows things aren't

working out, they aren't going to call me and say, "Hey Mark, let's face it. I'm not living up to expectations around here, so I think you should fire me." So, it's up to me as the leader to do something about it. I have to protect the rest of my team as well as do what's right for that individual. Letting them go will free them up for a job that may suit them much better. I always need to remind myself in these situations that it's not about me; it's about enabling the team to be as successful as they possibly can.

I remember a super nice guy I met not too long ago who had a decent-sized business. Much like the rest of us, he treated his business like a baby, except he was a complete maniac about it. He didn't trust anybody other than himself to do anything. It was disturbingly similar to overprotective parenting. Doting over your kids' every move is fine while they're babies and even when they get a little older, but you don't want them sucking their thumb on their way to freshman orientation at college.

This particular business owner had a bad hiring process, which led to stagnation of his business for more than two decades. The flaws with the way he onboarded people were numerous. He always hired the wrong people to do the wrong thing. There was no trust, and he didn't take the time to discover their strengths and weaknesses, so he just threw them into whatever role he thought he needed at the time without empowering them enough to succeed at it.

The result was always the same, which was that he fired them almost as hastily as he hired them. Some of us may go through a learning process like that for the first five years of our business, but this business owner has been repeating the same mistakes and flawed processes for more than twenty-two years.

It's important to spot any obvious flaws in your process and learn from the mistakes. Eventually, the number of lessons learned from the number of mistakes made will add up to a more refined process. That is how you will empower your team members with sufficient knowledge, address their strengths, and put them in a position to succeed.

A-LIST TALENT: WHAT DO THEY LOOK LIKE?

You might not even know what A-list talent looks like until you start hiring people. I didn't. In fact, I totally effed up the first A-lister I hired on my team.

I've been mentioning A-list talent a lot in this book, like it's an abundant resource just milling around employment offices across the country, waiting to be picked up by needy entrepreneurs and business leaders everywhere. It's not! In fact, A-list talent is extremely difficult to find.

Think of them like Major League Baseball all-stars. It's impossible to have a team full of them because there just aren't that many of them, some of them already play (work) for other teams (companies), and they're usually the highest-paid players (workers) in the game (industry). The other point is very few of those baseball all-stars start out as all-stars. Most of them begin their careers in the minor leagues, work their way up the system, and need to develop their skills at the pro level even further before they become all-stars. The same thing happens to most A-list talent in a business. They have to learn the business first, as well as their roles and responsibilities. Then they need to grow into future success. At that point, they may be ready to start exceeding expectations by a wide margin, which is when you know you have an A-list player on your team. As I mentioned earlier, it's up to you to empower your people to get better at what they do. You need to nurture their process of becoming A-listers by giving them the right tools, training, coaching, leadership, and more. They are a big part of your success and vice-versa.

The first assistant I hired—Vanessa—totally rocked. She stepped up in every way I could have imagined. Unfortunately, I was an immature business owner, and I foolishly thought I needed to pay less and get more out of people. At the time, I was looking for mules, not magicians, and that's a big difference!

Vanessa was a magician, and I treated her very badly, much more like a mule, and I've regretted it ever since.

Instead of recognizing her for her accomplishments and paying her accordingly, I squeezed her for much more than I ever should have. I did such a poor job as her leader that she eventually got fed up and justifiably left, but at least I realized it when it happened, and I'll never make that same mistake again.

I experienced a weird sort of premonition the night before she left. It wasn't any ghostly image I saw or anything bonkers like that, but I felt seriously ill that night. It was probably the result of a big ball of stress that developed in my stomach from being worried about Vanessa quitting.

I remember telling my wife that night, "I'm not entirely sure why, but I really feel like Vanessa is going to quit."

Deena said, "Cut it out. She's been with you for years. Why would she quit now?"

I replied, "I don't know, but something just isn't right."

Eventually, I fell asleep, but when I woke up and looked at my computer, which is what I always did in those days and had to immediately log in every morning, I saw her email that told me she had resigned.

That whole situation could have been avoided if I was a better business owner at the time. If I would have just paid her appropriately, she might have stayed on with me for many more years. But I can't do anything about the past, so I did the only thing I could do about it—I learned from it. We're all human, so we're going to make mistakes. As long as you learn from those mistakes and adjust accordingly, you will become a much better business owner. Especially in the hiring process.

Don't cheap out on people. Don't expect A-list talent to be happy being treated poorly or being paid C-List salaries. My mistake with Vanessa taught me that the idea of getting more for less with people is wrong. Now, I'm always thinking about how to pay people more because I know it's going to have the effect of helping the business grow, and it's very personally satisfying to be able to reward people for their efforts. I just wish I had that mindset from the beginning.

As a business owner, the team is a reflection of you, so it is 100 percent your fault if and when you hire bad people. But it's just a learning curve that we all go through.

MOVE EXISTING TALENT TO SUIT THEIR STRENGTHS

As leaders, not only do we need to recognize when people are doing a great job and pay them accordingly, but we also need to know where their best value is to the company. It's okay to move people around if you feel they're better suited for a different position.

Take the time to get to know your people. Find out what they enjoy doing, what they're great at, and what their Unique Ability is. Better yet, understand what their goals are. Find out where they want to be in one year, three years, or more. You might discover that some of your team members are not in the role that aligns best with their strengths. Therefore, you're not getting maximum value out of them, and they're not getting maximum value from their career.

FROM SOLID ASSISTANT TO SALES SUPERSTAR

We had another assistant at one time who was also excellent in her role. She worked for me for a while performing various administrative tasks on a daily basis, but one day, we discovered she also had a hidden talent for sales. We were having a conversation about a salesperson, and my assistant somewhat bullishly said, "I can do better than her!" I paused for a moment or two because whenever somebody makes a statement like that, I don't want to just dismiss the idea without due diligence. I want to find out if there is something I've overlooked, and perhaps an opportunity for shared success is presenting itself.

After thinking about it, it occurred to me that she did have some qualities that might actually make her a damned good salesperson, so I looked her in the eye and said, "Let's do it!"

Strangely enough, she wasn't very surprised by my willingness to let her accept the challenge. She didn't hesitate and got right to work when the time came. Sure enough, she not only outperformed the salesperson she originally called out, but she blew her completely out of the water. It wasn't even a contest. In fact, she quickly became our number-one salesperson.

This golden opportunity for an A-list salesperson was under my nose the whole time. She just wasn't in the right role. By keeping an open mind and empowering her to take on more, the team got a great salesperson, and she got a new, extremely rewarding career.

FROM SOLID SALESPERSON TO SUPERSTAR ASSISTANT

I've also seen the opposite situation take place, where we had a salesperson with a hidden talent for administrative work, and there is absolutely zero wrong with that. Kudos to the person with enough self-awareness to step away from a more lucrative position to something different, where they may not make as much money but where they will perform much better and be happier for it. Remember, money is not necessarily the master motivator for everyone or even most people.

This person was in sales for about six months, and I don't think I talked to her even once while she was there, as I'm not in the office and the team at this point is growing. After I did speak with her, I realized she was the type of person who never wanted to let you down. Helping people was what she lived for. If I gave her a list of ten things to do, she would not only have them done before the deadline, but they would be done to a level that consistently exceeded expectations. That's a kick-ass, superstar assistant, which is exactly who this person was.

If we hadn't kept our eyes open to the possibility of moving her from sales to administrative work, I would have had an underperforming salesperson who we may have had to let go at some point, and she would have been miserable while working at a job she didn't have the skills for. Instead, we got a great assistant, and she felt much more comfortable doing a job she was great at.

In the end, both situations ended up being a win-win for everybody involved. Constant management of a team member's strengths and weaknesses can only lead to better things for the entire team. I'm so happy with my team as it is currently constructed that I would unquestionably take them with me wherever I go, but I won't be afraid to continue looking for strengths and weaknesses within each of them to put them in positions where they can be most successful.

MONEY IS NOT THE MASTER MOTIVATOR

Managing the strengths and weaknesses of your team will always be a key factor in driving performance, but so is motivation, and you might be surprised to learn what motivates people the most. It's probably not what you think it is, and there is only one way to find out: ask.

I've discovered that money is not the master motivator most entrepreneurs think it is. Most nonentrepreneurial types want enough money to live comfortably and be able to do a few things they enjoy doing, like going to a concert or a sports event and out to a nice dinner once in a while.

Most people are motivated much more by things other than money. I've learned that striving for personal goals can actually be the biggest motivating factor of all, like weight loss, reconnecting with family and friends, or feeling like they're having a positive impact on the world.

Discovering the personal goals of your various team members doesn't need to be a mystery. The best approach is often the most direct, so I send out a six-month email to everyone on my team to find out what motivates them. It usually reads something like this:

> I hope you've all had an amazing half-year. I'm working on some really big things right now, and of course none of it would be possible without all your hard work

> and tremendous dedication. Thank you so much for everything! I appreciate the massive contributions you make to our shared success as a team.
>
> I also wanted to take this opportunity to check in and make sure I'm doing everything I can—as a leader—to contribute to your individual success as well.
>
> What are your personal, financial, and business goals?
>
> Remember, no dream is too big or too small, and I promise I won't judge you in any way. Also, rest assured that whatever information you choose to share with me will remain absolutely private, unless you want to share it with others as well.
>
> Feel free to let me know about anything else that's important in your life if you think I can help in any way. I will always care about you all a great deal, and I'm looking forward to working together to complete another year of incredible results. Thanks again—You rock!

Initially, most people don't know what their goals are because they don't have them. A lot of people just don't think about them. That's another reason why an exercise like this can be so beneficial to the team. It gets people thinking about goals.

The first two or three times they do this, most people have pretty vanilla goals. They're usually something like, "I want to get free from debt," or "I want to take a vacation somewhere warm." After that, however, a lot of people really get into it and start setting some great goals. Oddly, those goals are almost never about money. Some people tell me how much weight they want to lose or that they want to start a garden.

It's interesting for me to read what people list for goals because it helps me to learn a lot about the personalities on the team. It also helps me to understand what makes them tick. From there, I can usually find something really great that keeps them happily motivated.

For example, one person on the team wrote that she wanted to see her sister, whom she hadn't seen in a long time. I thought it would be especially cool if we spent a couple hundred dollars on a plane ticket for her sister, so that's what we did. It seemed like a fairly small thing because it certainly didn't cost much, but my team member didn't see it that way. She absolutely loved it!

The plane ticket idea was something I could have only implemented by getting to know my team. Different things motivate different people, and sometimes incredibly satisfying goals can be easily achieved just by getting to know your team. As a business owner, this sort of gesture creates real loyalty. Think about this: In a previous job, did anyone ever ask what your goals were? If so, and they helped you achieve them, what did that do to your loyalty? Probably quite a bit.

CHAPTER NINE

LETTING GO

If you want to do a few small things right, do them yourself. If you want to do great things and make a big impact, learn to delegate.

—JOHN C. MAXWELL, AMERICAN AUTHOR, SPEAKER, AND LEADERSHIP EXPERT

The bottom line of your business will likely take a small hit when you first start hiring people. It's a natural occurrence because you need to take time away from what you're great at to invest in hiring, training, and managing your talent. Empowering people to succeed takes time, but the ROI on this is going to be huge...someday. In the beginning, you might expect to lose around 10 to 20 percent of your revenue.

What's important is that you stay focused on letting go. Have a good vision of how the company is going to grow based on the hiring you're doing. In the last chapter, we talked all about how to motivate people by learning what their goals are. Now, it's up to you to set your own goals so you don't lose focus and get tempted to steer away from hiring by something as shortsighted as a 20 percent loss in revenue during the initial process.

When you're a solopreneur, there's only one person. If you hire one person, you're doubling the impact. Therefore, if you're a big company with a lot of employees and you hire one person, you're not impacting nearly as much. During the initial hiring process, the effects depend on the size of your company.

Different new-hires are also going to have different impacts. Mailroom personnel, salespeople, executives, and assistants all have varying levels of impact on your business and they're all in different areas of your business, so you need to be aware of how impactful each new-hire could become.

I'm not a hiring expert, but there are plenty of great books that have been written about hiring great people. For example, *How to Hire A-Players: Finding the Top People for Your Team- Even If You Don't Have a Recruiting Department* by Eric Herrenkohl is an excellent choice.

When I talk about hiring A-listers, I'm just sharing some insight about what I've learned from past experience.

Hopefully, it will help you to get a jump start that I didn't have on hiring great team members.

SETTING GOALS

I just want to be clear that I'm not a goal-setting expert, but I've read a lot about the subject, and I've taken a lot of goal-setting courses. What I've learned is that there are a variety of ways to set goals, and different methods work for different people.

A lot of people have found success with the SMART method, which is an acronym that represents Specific, Measurable, Achievable, Relevant, and Time-limited. Plenty of resources are available to help you pursue this approach if you're interested in learning more about it.

Whether you pursue the SMART goals method or not, I strongly recommend doing your own research on goal-setting and perhaps finding an expert in the field to help you with it.

Although I'm no expert, I have learned a few things about goal-setting that have worked for me. For instance, I've learned the shorter, the better when setting goals. I don't set them five years out because they don't seem real enough when they're that far away. Goal-setting too far in the future allows procrastination to creep in.

I prefer to keep most of my goals to ninety days, but I know others who are successful in planning them for a full year. Any longer than that, however, and I fear they become too abstract to be effective for me. Goals are going to be different for everybody, but some of them could be as simple as the following:

- I want to be the biggest business owner in my region.
- In the next ninety days, I want to generate X amount of revenue.
- Within sixty days, I will hire an assistant and a marketing specialist.
- In ninety days, I want to leave the business for a month.
- I want to shift focus from 100 percent on daily operations to 40 to 50 percent on creating growth.

The last one is a good starting point because it's extremely valuable, and it's doable right now. Sometimes it's helpful to reframe goals as questions because that gets your mind searching for answers on how to complete them. In this case, I recommend rephrasing that last goal as, "How do I shift 100 percent of my focus on daily operations to 40 to 50 percent on creating growth?"

I'm not saying don't have five-year goals, but I am saying that the shorter goals are, the more real they become, and they definitely work better for me. For example, the entire creation of this book began with one question I wrote down just nine months before the book was released on June 19. That question was, "How can I share my knowledge, experience, and lessons learned in business to the world, have it done by June 19, and give all the money to charity? That was my nine-month goal, I had no clue how to make that happen at that moment, but it allowed me to set the wheels in motion. Producing a book involves a very tight timeline, but setting a real date played a big role in making it happen.

THINK

Think deeply about how you can accomplish that goal. Hiring the right people in the right places will always be one way to do it. Once you're able to do that, you'll be able to transform most of your thinking away from routine tasks and managing people to enhancing your vision and growing the company.

People lose sight of how valuable the act of thinking is. I can accomplish a hell of a lot just by sitting on the beach with my family and smoking a cigar. I'm relaxing and enjoying time with my family, but I'm also using that time to think about growing the business. Some of my best ideas happen that way. They also happen when I'm drinking coffee in the morning, in the shower, at the gym. Idea generation happens for me while I'm doing all these other activities because my mind isn't bogged down with the tedium of administrative items. Besides, administrative tasks aren't in my job description as a leader, but setting goals, creating vision, and growing the company definitely are.

I try to dedicate at least half of my day exclusively to thinking deeply about my business. Productive thoughts might happen while listening to a podcast, reading a book, or doing nothing more than smoking a cigar. A fifteen-minute meditation to clear my mind may produce some valuable thinking as well. It doesn't matter how you're thinking as long as you're doing it. Back in the day, I always thought the only way to be productive was to be busy. I wasn't aware of the enormous value and productivity of thinking.

There is a societal misconception with this that's a little confusing to me, but most people think if you're not physically working, you're lazy. The act of thinking or brainstorming isn't socially acknowledged as "real work." I disagree with that sentiment wholeheartedly.

DM DAY: MY HACK FOR THINKING

People love the idea of life hacks, which Google defines as "a strategy or technique adopted in order to manage one's time and daily activities in a more efficient way." A life hack that I've had a lot of success with is something I call "DM Day."

DM Day is a day that is all about me. I go to a resort or other peaceful place like a park, beach, or such by myself, and I completely unplug. There is no smartphone, tablet, or laptop with me. It's just me with a pad of paper, a pen, and some serious thinking.

This getaway gives me an opportunity to come up with some ideas about how to be a better leader, help my team more, and execute my power focus to a higher level. I also start thinking about where my company is, what my pain points are, where some areas of untapped value are, and other big picture ideas. When I come up with an idea I like, I write it down, and I take it with me. When DM Day is done, I usually have some great ideas to test and a great reset to continue focusing on what's important.

It felt very strange when I first started taking these DM Days—almost as if I was stealing from my business by not being in it. I felt selfish, which in a weird way, I guess was true, but is there anything wrong with that? If you commit to something like this for yourself, you'll notice a lot of amazing doors open up, and you'll likely realize some tremendous clarity, just like I did.

A CUSTOM-TAILORED CASE STUDY

I firmly believe that you, as a business owner, can let go no matter what industry you're in. It doesn't matter if you're in real estate, automotive repair, high-end tailoring, or anything else in between. You can still think deeply, establish goals, and let go to make more money and have an exponentially better quality of life.

For instance, I recently had a conversation about letting go with my friend Tim, who is also my tailor (a very high-end one) who has a lot of business owners, athletes, celebrities, and other people with large disposable income as clients.

The conversation was set in motion when my COO, Peter, and I were at the Four Seasons in Palm Beach on a two-day business retreat. We were doing some brainstorming, and Peter mentioned that he wanted to have some suit jackets tailored, so I said, "I know just the guy," and I texted Tim.

As usual, Tim immediately texted me back, saying he would meet us at the resort. So, Peter and I kicked back, sipping on tropical drinks in perfect weather with the blue-green waves providing an unbelievably aesthetic backdrop to our brainstorming session while Tim, who is an absolute rock-star tailor, was busting his ass to meet us there personally.

But as we were chilling out, I thought better of Tim going out of his way to meet us then and there, so I texted him, "Tim, why the hell are you meeting us here?" He ignored me, so my question went nowhere. Truthfully, there was no reason why Tim shouldn't have been there chilling with us, not working, but just basking in the sunshine. The problem was that Tim was still caught up in a micromanager, business-owner mentality. He refused to ever let anything go and claimed that his business was all about the personal touch.

At that time, if you were a client of Tim's, he would arrive at your doorstep to measure you, remeasure you, deliver shirts and pants, and make sure you were deliriously happy with all of his service. It's outstanding service, and I would never refer to it in any other way because he's great at it. However, it's not scalable to any level other than exactly the one he was at, and that's not necessary either. Unfortunately for Tim, his outstanding service also came at a great cost to his personal life.

When I spoke with Tim sometime later, we had a back-and-forth with him arguing that running all over Florida, doing everything by himself with no help was essential to providing the level of service required for his business to excel. The funny thing is that it was nothing I wouldn't have said when I was a micromanaging maniac too, circa 2005. But it didn't stop me from debating my point with him.

"BS!" I told him. "When Oprah Winfrey checks in at a Four Seasons resort, do you think the company president flies across the world to personally check her in and bring her bags to her room?"

Tim smiled just a little.

So, I asked him, "What are your goals—your dreams for the business?"

It turned out that he had a very clear vision of what he wanted for his company. He gave me some real data to describe his goals for the business. The problem was that it was impossible for him to get there in the way he was going about it. He was trading time for dollars, and he would have needed about thirty-six working hours per day to reach the numbers he was describing to me. Remember, time is extremely valuable, and with that business model, Tim didn't have enough of it.

I needed to be sure that Tim knew I wasn't trying to beat him up with my insight. Instead, I tried to show him some tough love because I cared about him and wanted him to achieve everything he deserved. After hearing his goals and explaining that they were unattainable with his current business model, I explained how he could actually reach the numbers he dreamed of. "You need to hire some help. Pay someone thirty dollars or whatever it takes to do a great job measuring people. Sit down with them and conduct a serious interview to make sure they're professional and they know what the hell they're doing. When you find the person who seems like the right choice, make sure you're confident about their abilities and how they're going to represent your business."

I thought it might help him to know that I practice what I preach. "That's how we've been doing inspections at my company since 2005," I said.

He still wasn't buying it though, so he volleyed back, "Well, what about having people running around everywhere, delivering clothing?"

I replied, "Seriously, I get things delivered from Amazon every day. You can have items shipped through a bunch of different companies. Try them all and use the one you like best."

Tim's situation is trickier than most because, in one way, his unbelievable attention to detail and excellent service is what makes him so great. But in another way, sometimes it's more inconvenient to the customer than it is great service. Sometimes it's great when he personalizes his service because he hangs out with me, we have some good conversation, and it's like meeting up with an old friend. Other times, however, I'm so busy that I just want to avoid the social gathering and get my suits so I can get things done.

Let the business owner who is happy with the status quo continue doing everything himself and having virtually no time to enjoy his nonbusiness life. That's a high-paying job though—not a real business. Those people aren't looking for more. Tim, however, had vision. He had thoughtfully planned goals and dreamed of a bigger business, but the only way that was going to happen was if he let go of some of the lesser tasks, like delivering clothing and measuring everybody.

He probably billed about two to three million dollars of business per year. Based on what I already know about him and his business, if he let go and focused on growth, I could easily see him turning his revenue numbers into $20 million annually in two years or less.

After I pleaded my case to Tim about how to achieve real growth and fulfill his vision in his business, I told him that not only would he make more money, but he'd have more free time to spend with his family.

He replied, "Yes, but Mark I'm actually home around six or seven every night. I put the kids to bed, and sure, I go back into the office from ten o'clock to three in the morning."

That's when I just about lost it. I said, "You've got to be kidding me! You think that's enough time to be home?"

He started to get defensive, "Well, you don't understand. I catch problems by doing a lot of double-checking in my office."

I told him, "Tim, there are websites like Upwork now where you can find a virtual worker to go over those numbers for you. It's not a lot of money, and it might give you an extra hour or two at home with your wife and kids, instead of being in the office with the door locked. Not only that, but the Upwork person you hire will probably do a way better job than you because after working eighteen-hour days, you must be missing a few errors here and there. A virtual worker double-checking your system will actually save you some money by not making costly mistakes."

That's when it finally hit him. "Holy shit, I never really thought about it like that! Sometimes I'm so damned tired that the numbers start getting blurry, and I don't even know what I'm looking at by the end of the night. Plus, if I hire really good people to interact with the customers, the service won't suffer either. It's not like my name has to be attached to every pair of pants that gets cut and tapered."

WORK-LIFE HARMONY

I think something that resonated particularly well with Tim at that moment was that not only could his business grow to where he knew it could, but the idea of being able to spend more quality time at home with his family struck him as well. He realized that perhaps his business could grow while his personal life grew as well.

Tim had two big problems. One was that his business couldn't grow based on the model he was implementing, but perhaps even more importantly was that he didn't have any quality time with his family. Some people would say he had no work-life balance. I would argue that a different term is more appropriate.

The concept of a work-life "balance" doesn't work for me because I don't think it tells the whole story. I think you need to strive for a work-life "harmony" because there is a big difference between balance and harmony. To me, "balance" indicates you're in the office for half your day and at home for the other half, which is great, but what's more important is what you're doing when you're home.

When you're home, are you playing with the kids, making dinner with your wife, and having a family night, or are you in your home office with the door locked—like Tim was—staring at your computer screen trying to solve business problems? The latter situation, although you're technically at home, is not harmonious in any way. Sure, you've got balance, but what good is that?

A lot of business owners try to get away with it. They'll say something like, "Well, I'm at home all day, so I have work-life balance." That could be true, but most of them are up at the crack of dawn staring at spreadsheets and staying in their office until late at night with only small breaks for meals and bathroom visits.

Of course, the opposite could be true as well. Some people who claim work-life balance might be sitting at home, watching television, and chain-eating bags of Cool Ranch Doritos. That's not healthy either, and it's definitely not a recipe for business success.

Working hard is important, but you can work hard in less time too. Remember, it is possible to work harder *and* smarter. For instance, if you go home with some critical business issue hanging over your head so much that you can't enjoy any of your downtime, there is no harmony in that either. In that case, you're much better off staying at work for an extra hour or two to finish the job the right way. Otherwise, you're too distracted while you're at home thinking about what's waiting for you in your business.

There's no shame in working hard. In fact, just the opposite is true. I'm a better husband, father, friend, and all-around person because I love what I do, I'm great at it, and it allows me to help others. That's got nothing to do with balance.

As business owners, we tend to gravitate toward doing everything ourselves because our egos refuse to allow us to believe that we can let go and delegate. We don't allow ourselves to think that someone we hire could possibly do something as well as we can. When I was doing that, I realized it was time to push my ego aside, work harder *and* smarter, and I found my work-life harmony.

CHAPTER TEN

PAY YOURSELF!

The art is not in making money, but in keeping it.

—PROVERB

In my days as a micromanaging business owner, doing everything including paperwork, marketing, and refilling the water cooler, there was one thing I wasn't doing, which was paying myself a salary.

For almost nine years, I used my business account like it was my personal piggy bank, which is irresponsible on both a personal and business level. At one point, I found myself in Columbus, Ohio, buying yet another car that I didn't need. There was no structure in place to account for how much money my business was making or spending, nor was there any control over the effect my personal expenses had on my business. I remember thinking, "Did I have enough money to buy this car?" I did, but I was drawing from my business account to do it.

Sometimes my business account would have a decent chunk of money in it, but other times, it would sink like a box of rocks to the bottom of the ocean. That level of financial instability caused me to get stressed out and even depressed because I was also working damned hard and putting in a ton of hours. That's a downright mentally debilitating place to be.

You're riding too many emotions at the same time when there's no separation. It's like being on the world's largest roller coaster with no safety harness in place. Not only are you in a constant fray of ups and downs, but you're also flying all over the place at the same time.

Finally, I came up with a plan to create some structure and gain a little control over my business and personal bank accounts. I decided to pay myself $1,000 per month in the beginning. It started out as a test run, similar to what I did later by going to Florida for a month. I wanted to see what would happen to my company's profits if I paid myself a salary every month. Worst case scenario: I could loan it back the same day if I needed to, but I still set up an automatic payment to myself, just to make sure I didn't get tempted to continue winging it.

A strange thing happened when I paid myself a salary. It gave me a separation of emotional attachments. Previously, I noticed that when everything is riding on one account, your financial security becomes an emotional roller coaster with some really cool climbs, but also some nasty, stomach-churning dips. When I separated my bank accounts, however, I noticed myself getting more excited when both accounts grew drastically. A structure was in place for me to control them, and my financial life and emotional health were both better for it.

With both accounts growing so consistently, I started to increase my salary. Initially, I gave myself a small raise to $3,000 per month. After I saw how well that was going, I increased it to $10,000. It didn't take long before I realized how powerful this was and was able to pay myself a decent chunk per month, still seeing tremendous growth in the business account.

Once you learn how to separate your personal finances from your business, you'll see how much smoother your life can get. If having no separation is like a roller coaster ride without safety harnesses, separation is like being on the merry-go-round with all the horses equipped with air bags in their heads. Moreover, you don't have a real business if you don't pay yourself.

If the idea of paying yourself is starting to make sense (and it should), keep reading because there is a great resource to dig deeper on the subject at the end of the next section.

YOUR BUSINESS IS A BIG DEAL. RUN IT LIKE ONE

You're running a business, not some cardboard-cutout lemonade stand on your parents' front lawn. Grow up and run your business like the big deal it is. Excuse the tough love attitude, but if you couldn't tell by now, it's kind of my thing.

Most entrepreneurs I know run their business out of their bank accounts. By that, I mean if they have $100,000 in their bank account, they're feeling pretty good about things. On the other hand, if they have $5,000 in their bank account, it's time to panic. They start freaking out and doing something just for the sake of doing it. That is when bad things can happen to good businesses because poor decisions made in the spur of the moment can change everything.

I challenge you to try paying yourself for six months. Chances are, you'll think it's awesome for the first month or two. Things will usually tighten up around the third or fourth month. That's when you could become susceptible to panic mode again. If that happens, do your best to harness your emotions. Meditate, breathe deeply, and do whatever it takes to get back in the moment, relax, and stay with the plan. Continue paying yourself for the next few months, and don't make any rash decisions about whether or not you want to continue doing it until the six months are up.

We all have a certain monthly dollar figure we need to live on before our habits become wasteful. What that figure is depends on the level of success you're at. If you need $10,000 per month to pay the bills and do the things you want to do, you can give yourself a salary of $25,000 and feel very comfortable. That takes all the stress out of the situation because your salary stays the same no matter what happens in that situation. At that point, all you care about is if your business is making more money because you also know that you don't need any more money in your personal account to live comfortably.

Financial stress is brutal. It's a marriage killer, and it's a great way to give yourself a stroke. You don't need to live day-to-day without having any control over your personal and business bank accounts. Make it a goal to pay yourself. It will free you from all that financial stress, and you'll feel completely removed from the rat race, which is the whole reason most of us got into business in the first place. There is a great book to learn more about this. It's called, *Profit First: Transform Your Business from a Cash-Eating Monster to a Money-Making Machine,* by Mike Michalowicz

WHAT HAPPENS NEXT?

Unfortunately, I've known plenty of entrepreneurs who have been in business for ten, twenty years, or more, and still don't take a salary. They have all the ups and downs of their bank accounts I mentioned. Worse than that, they eat stress for breakfast, lunch, and dinner. Their marriages are in jeopardy and so is their state of mind and overall health. It's not an ideal way to live, and it doesn't have to be that way.

A guy named John approached me a few years ago wanting to pick my brain about a few things. He had a big lifestyle and wasn't thrilled with getting a realistic handle on how much money he was actually spending, which was a decent amount. His business was doing well though—about $70,000 net per month.

I asked him, "How much of that do you pay yourself in salary?" That's usually one of the first questions I ask an entrepreneur who says they're doing well.

He replied, "Oh, I don't pay myself anything consistently. I just sort of take money out whenever I need it."

Once again, I began my approach with, "John, do you want me to shoot straight with you or sugarcoat it?"

He said, "Of course, I need you to shoot straight. Go for it."

I started, "I hear that kind of nonsense about just taking money whenever you need it every day. Don't take this the wrong way, because I'm just being honest and trying to help, but it's the dumbest thing I've ever heard. Here's what you need to do." I explained to him how paying himself a salary would take the stress out of everything for him.

He fought it for a while, saying, "Yeah, yeah. I'll get to it. I hear what you're saying."

Several months later, he finally bought in to what I was telling him and was able to pull enough money from his growing business to comfortably afford the lifestyle he wanted. Better yet, he also told me that his wife began to share his excitement about the growth of his business because she could see the fruits of his labor from the financial separation he created.

You'll notice somewhat of an inner peace when you pay yourself a salary. There's a calm involved when you understand that you can have the lifestyle you want and that it doesn't have to be stressful. Paying yourself a salary is a big step in the right direction of the evolution of your leadership.

SUSTAINING GROWTH

Why do the majority of lottery winners go broke? It's usually because they have no idea what to do with the money when they get it. Lottery winners generally don't understand how to protect their money, how to grow it, or how to preserve it.

If you're not cutting yourself a salary and just running your business by the seat of your pants, you're not that far removed from a lottery winner. You don't have the structure in place to control your business and personal life. That's okay, however, because you're like most business owners. You just need to learn from that mistake and evolve so your business and you can sustain growth.

Sustainability requires constantly enhancing your knowledge of financial awareness. Sure, there's a lot to learn, but you're always learning anyway. Once you start making more money, your thoughts start to turn toward your legacy because you're probably in business for more reasons than just your own financial well-being. You may have a spouse, kids, grandchildren, and others to think about. Even if there isn't a family legacy to consider, you probably have some charities you like to help out with all your hard work.

The secret to sustaining growth and evolving as a business leader isn't solely about money. It's about knowledge and implementation. You can make plenty of money, but what good is it if it's just wasted? It's not what you make. It's what you keep, grow, and steward.

In the final chapter, I'll detail what it means to "knowledge-up" in the real world. If you're serious about building wealth for life and finding true freedom, this is a crucial concept. It's not about formal education. Rather, to knowledge-up is about smartly using online resources, finding the right mentors, and maintaining awareness. The more you know, the more opportunities you'll have to sustain growth.

CHAPTER ELEVEN

KNOWLEDGE-UP

NEVER STOP INVESTING IN YOURSELF. YOU'RE WORTH IT!

Formal education will make you a living. Self-education will make you a fortune.

—JIM ROHN, AMERICAN ENTREPRENEUR, AUTHOR, AND MOTIVATIONAL SPEAKER

Way before I became a remote business owner and even before I was a micromanaging maniac, I was an eighteen-year-old kid in Columbus, Ohio, desperately in search of real knowledge to make real money, so I took action. I went on a road trip to knowledge-up.

There I was—in 1996—young and broke but hungry to learn from the best in the world. I was in a room full of people, all much older than I was, waiting for a real estate infomercial guy named Russ to enter the room and share the secrets of his success with us. It was a make-or-break moment for me because I spent every last dime I had to make this trip.

It was the first time I had ever left my family for that long, so that part was scary enough, but fortunately, my dreams were always bigger than my obstacles. So I made the twenty-plus-hour road trip from Columbus to Cape Coral, Florida, in an old, beat-up Chevy S-10 pickup truck. I didn't even have enough money left over for a room to stop and get a nap before I arrived at the hotel in Cape Coral or any sort of reasonable nutrition, so I slept in that truck (mostly, with one eye open) and ate predominantly candy bars and junk food on the way down there. Yes, the sleep requirements and nutritional needs of an ambitious eighteen-year-old are quite different from that of a been-there-done-that forty-something.

I sat in the front row of that room because I was there to learn. Honestly, I was fully committed to learning whatever Russ had to say that day. He shared some basic information and then said, "Let's jump right in and start making deals happen!" He pulled out the newspaper and went to the real estate listings and said, "Here we go," and started making calls. For those of you too young to remember, way back in 1996, most real estate listings were in the newspaper, not online. A woman answered one of his phone calls, and told Russ that she and her husband were getting a divorce and they needed to sell the house quickly. She went on to say that she knew what the house was worth and what she would accept for a sale price if she could close the deal within seven days.

Immediately after hearing his conversation, I thought, "Holy shit, I can do that! I'm going to make millions." Dumbfounded by how much of a no-brainer this approach seemed, I took a look around the room, expecting to see the same level of interest I had in everyone else's face as well, but I didn't see that. Instead, I saw a room full of men and women in their thirties and older talking about what to get for lunch and where to go for beers after the presentation was over. Meanwhile, I was thinking, "I spent my life savings of $2,500 to get here. I'm going to learn how this guy is successful and replicate it to the best of my ability."

Just then, I gathered as many bags of Doritos and Cheetos for lunch and dinner from the vending machine as I could, and headed back to my room with a newspaper to start making some calls. All I had to do was have a similar conversation to the one Russ showed us with the right person. What he was doing gave me the confidence I needed to see how a professional went about doing business. The real magic was in making the calls, and I knew I could do that. For some reason, I know a lot of people who just learn with no intention of actually carrying out the lesson, but if you're anything like me, you're excited to put what you learn into action. All of a sudden, real estate investing wasn't just a theory; it was a reality.

At the time, I was just a dopey kid who heard about different ways to make money, which may have given me ideas and dreams, but now I had actual knowledge to make some of those things happen.

That was a great way for a young kid to get started, but there's also a lesson to be learned from that for experienced business leaders as well. To knowledge-up is important for all of us. You're never too old to continue learning. As entrepreneurs, we can all get to a certain level of success, but none of us get into business to be mediocre or average. We get into business because we want to be exceptional, and to be exceptional, you have to keep growing, which means you need to knowledge-up.

JOIN A MASTERMIND GROUP

There's a reason the rich get richer. It's because they're always talking with each other and growing. They knowledge-up because they're not satisfied unless they're growing. *Think and Grow Rich* by Napoleon Hill includes in-depth explanations of how some of the most successful people in the history of the world do this by forming mastermind groups.

Mastermind groups are positively invaluable in my mind. Picture a room full of twenty extremely successful people, each with their own unique strengths—some may be great at marketing, while others may be great salespeople, and still others might be incredible innovators. Within that room, everybody shares why they're great at what they do and how they do it. Do you think you might learn a few things from being in a room like that? Absolutely, you will. Not only will you knowledge-up in a big way, but you'll also expedite your growth significantly.

One of the greatest aspects of mastermind groups is that they're not just beneficial in terms of receiving knowledge, but they also provide satisfaction for people who can share knowledge. In one way, you may receive a great tip on how to solve a particular problem in your business, but you may also be able to share some of your expertise to help somebody else out. It's a win-win like no other.

See what others say about the mastermind by going to www.10MinuteBusinessOwner.com/Mastermind

YOU'RE NOT ALONE

Mastermind groups are full of so much experience that it actually helps to be the dumbest guy in the room. That is when you'll learn the most. You might show up to a mastermind group with one or two big problems that you know are plaguing your bottom line, but you don't know how to fix it. Guess what? You're not alone.

Chances are, one or more people in that mastermind group have struggled with the same problem(s) you're currently facing. If you get the answer to a big problem, then participation in that group will have saved you excessive time because, otherwise, you'll either have to continue wrestling with the problem yourself or hire your way out of it. Both of those options will take considerably longer than just stepping into a room filled with greatness and getting the answer.

The biggest value of masterminding is the emotional side of it. Connecting and talking to people who get it is extremely helpful because other people don't understand what we're going through on most days. Being a business owner or an entrepreneur also means living sort of a double life. We have to regularly flip from a business mentality to a family one, which can be mentally challenging and exhausting at times. That is something only other business owners or entrepreneurs can identify with and understand. They may even be able to speak from experience and provide some helpful insight for you.

That emotional connection is positively life-changing. Of course, mastermind groups can also help you to avoid costly mistakes and increase revenue. They're a great resource to share both successes and problems.

I've been doing masterminds since 2008, and I've seen the impact they can have on many levels. See what others are saying about them by going to www.10MinuteBusinessOwner.com/Mastermind

SHARE THE WEALTH

Who do you call first when you just closed a deal for $180,000? Grandma will think you're either making it up or not have any idea what you're talking about, and your friends from high school will just think you're bragging. Everybody in the mastermind group, however, will be able to share what that success really means.

What if that deal for $180,000 should have been worth $500,000? That is a problem that only exists in the entrepreneurial world, and you're not going to get any sympathy from Grandma or your friends. In fact, your friends might punch you for it. Once again, however, the mastermind group knows all about how that loss of $320,000 is keeping you up at night and how you can avoid it in the future. Proper perspective is everything, isn't it?

If you're not part of a mastermind group yet, find a good one and join now. If you want to continue growing your business, it's absolutely essential.

READ AND LISTEN

Beyond the huge impact a mastermind group can have, there are other ways to knowledge-up as well. For instance, I didn't read one book until after I graduated high school. Since then, I've probably read more than five thousand of them because there is so much knowledge I can get from them. *Think and Grow Rich* is a great one that I've read around one hundred times. Just like I mentioned earlier about being on the beach and thinking about my next big deal, you can also get on the treadmill for twenty minutes and read a book about business that can accelerate your knowledge.

Podcasts are another great resource for knowledge. If you have fifteen minutes of driving time between appointments, press play on the podcast app of your smartphone and knowledge-up while you're driving. Check out my podcast at www.10MinuteBusinessOwner.com/Podcast.

I also like *The MFCEO Project* with Andy Frisella, and Ed Mylett. They are business leaders who are sharing real knowledge that can exponentially accelerate your growth.

KNOWLEDGE, NOT EDUCATION

The key to bringing all these potential assets—masterminds (above all), books, podcasts, and anything else you can find—is to invest in yourself.

Never stop investing in yourself!

I've seen a lot of great business owners who think they've got it all figured out. Trust me, to this day, I've still never met anyone who really has it all figured out. Business is an always-changing journey. You need to get into a mastermind ASAP. Invest that $5,000 in yourself and realize you're worth it. If you're serious about your business, mastermind groups are a must.

The books and the podcasts require minimal investment, if any, in dollar terms. The masterminds may cost thousands of dollars, but the ROI will be well worth it. Personally, I've spent millions of dollars on mastermind groups, and I don't regret a penny of it because I know the value of them has been far greater for me.

As I'm writing this to you, I'm in two mastermind groups: one that runs $50,000 a year and another that runs $100,000 a year for three meetings.

I'm not saying you should start out at that level, but find a two-day mastermind where you can unplug and knowledge-up for $5,000 and invest in yourself.

I would be stealing from you right now if I didn't tell you about the mastermind where we meet three times per year. You can learn more about it by going to www.10MinuteBusinessOwner.com/Mastermind.

You may see some free masterminds along your journey to creating more money, time, and freedom from your business, but I don't recommend anything free at this level. Sure, you might pick up on a thing or two, but there is exponentially higher value in the mastermind groups that aren't free. Just like so many other things in life and business, you get what you pay for with mastermind groups as well.

The quote from Jim Rohn that begins this chapter is so true. Formal education is great at getting you a high-paying job, but that's not what leaders want. Leaders want to lead and, therefore, need to keep growing. Education stops after a four-year degree or maybe even a doctorate, but knowledge never stops. There is always something in a book or a podcast you can use, and a good mastermind is a continuous source of specialized knowledge from various high-quality resources.

Now is a good time to see how you've knowledged-up from reading this book. I commend you for taking the time to go through it in an effort to grow as a business leader. This is a good time to go back and see what pieces of knowledge have resonated particularly well with you from this book. You've probably highlighted some sections to make it easier for yourself. Just in case, I'll steer you in some good possible directions.

Most people are either going to pay attention to the notion of paying themselves, finding their no-tivation, investing in themselves, or knowing their data. There are plenty of other choices, but those are probably the most popular takeaways from this book. When you're done reviewing, create noticeable action steps you can take to get real results, so you can verify that what I've discussed here actually works.

Make sure to go to www.10MinuteBusinessOwner.com to see the expanded video versions of these pieces.

CONCLUSION

Wealth is the ability to fully experience life.

—HENRY DAVID THOREAU, AMERICAN POET AND PHILOSOPHER

I remember lying in bed at my parents' house in Ohio. I was a kid dreaming of a day when I would be rich, which at that age meant earning $100,000 per year. Fortunately for me, I wasn't *just* a dreamer. I always had the desire to make my dreams a reality. So, I did the math and quickly figured out that I had to make twenty dollars per hour and work around fourteen hours a day to get to $100,000 for the year.

The first few years, I didn't get close to my goal, but I knew I was on the right track because I saw plenty of opportunities along the way. The vision for my entrepreneurial journey was developing, and I knew as long as I kept growing, I would get to where I wanted to go.

Freedom was within reach. I would soon be able to do what I wanted, when I wanted, and how I wanted. And nobody could tell me any differently. No high school teachers would be lecturing me about getting a real job, and I would be able to take care of my family and friends who I cared about most.

Now, here I am, back to the island life, about to hop on a multi-million-dollar yacht with my family and friends for a week. As I'm finishing up the writing of this book, I'm thinking about some things—what I've given to be here, the years of hard work I've put in, the successes I've had, and the mistakes I've made. After all, not everything has been rainbows and unicorns. I've failed plenty, and I'll continue to fail, but that's okay because I learned a lot from every failure I experienced. It's been a long, crazy trip, and I'm so thankful I took it. I hope you do the same.

What's crazy is, today, I can easily spend the $100,000 I used to dream about as a dopey eighteen-year-old kid on marketing in one week. Yes, it's a different world I live in now, as my family and friends all prepare to have the chef serve lunch and the captain pull anchor to go out to sea. Maybe that sounds a little pretentious, but I've earned it. After all, I've already put in my ten minutes today (wink). Besides, gratitude definitely doesn't escape me because I remember how tough things can be in business and in life. I'm grateful for everything I have today and everyone around me, but I'm most grateful that I didn't give up on my dreams like many others do.

When tough times or problems occur in my business, I use a little hack I learned many years ago. It's helped me get through some of my toughest obstacles. I say, "Thank you! Thank you for this problem because it wouldn't be given to me if I couldn't handle it." Then, I smile and say, "Someday, this will make for a great Chapter Seven in a book I write because people who have everything handed to them have nothing to write about."

Gratitude is a very powerful tool. Yes, I'm on a yacht in the British Virgin Islands right now, which I'm super grateful for, just like when I was on a small boat on a thirty-acre lake in Ohio, enjoying the moment and knowing that I was in control of all my decisions.

Truthfully, I've put in plenty of fourteen-plus-hour days in my life. You probably have as well, but it doesn't really matter how much time you put in as long as you're thinking about your business and how to grow it while you're enjoying life.

The ultimate goal of this book is to give you an idea of what is possible. I haven't gone into every microdetail of running a successful business because there are already plenty of great books available to help you do that. I've mentioned some of them.

I know we've spent some time together at this point, and if you've made it this far, I commend you. Make sure to get to www.10MinuteBusinessOwner.com to see all the latest that's happening and get some free gifts just for stopping by.

I want to leave you with a 30,000-foot view of what is possible by doing one, two, or three of the most noticeable things I've done to achieve real, sustainable growth in my businesses and life. If a kid from small-town Ohio with big dreams and barely a high school diploma can do it, you can too. Bon voyage!

Mark Evans DM, Wife Deena, Son Mark III

ABOUT THE AUTHOR

MARK EVANS, aka "The Deal Maker" and "Digital Nomad," has become an industry icon for not only building a massive real estate empire but by the way he built it: by traveling the world and enjoying life to the fullest while delegating appropriately to A-list team members.

It all began with a period of trial and error. Could he run the business from anywhere in the world? Could he let go of the time-consuming routine aspects of his business? Could he sustain growth by working ten minutes per day on two massively successful businesses? Truthfully, he accomplished all that and more. Now, he wants to share the secrets to success with as many people as possible.

With his tough-love approach, Mark has already assisted other entrepreneurs and business leaders to spend less time *in* the business and more time *on* the business. He is also happy to mention that 100 percent of the net profits from this book are going to charity. The Caring House Project Foundation, Addison Quinn Foundation, and the Lorraine Boys and Girls Club are just a few of the organizations that he is happy to help.

Stay up-to-date with Mark Evans DM on social media:

- Facebook @markevansdm
- Instagram @markevansdm
- LinkedIn @markevansdm

Made in the USA
Middletown, DE
30 June 2022

68135876R00104